INTERLUDE

By Roo Phelps

INTERLUDE

Copyright © 2019 by Roo Phelps. All rights reserved.

ISBN: 978-1-6951-48031

Dedications

To: Charleen and Greg Phelps,
Who used to jokingly tell an overly dramatic
child, "Ya, ya, put it in the book."
The only words I'll ever have to write
for you will always be filled
with endless appreciation, adoration, love, and respect.

For:
My best friend Jesse,
who shows me every day that the joke
is funniest when life is not.
Let's spend a lifetime waving to each other's ships,
and showing up at each other's door.
Always.

"And all this time
I've been staring at the minute hand.
Oh what a crime
That I can't seem to understand,
That life is in the waiting."

- Kina Grannis

Prologue

I once knew a love that broke me.

It was a love that carried me high into the clouds, so high my vision was obscured in its mist. It dressed me up in clothes that didn't feel right. It dolled me up in makeup and boots. It asked and it took. It excused itself but never me. This love I clung to, like a giant rock on the shore, being battered against it unforgivingly again and again by the sea. This love called itself love, this love called itself caring, this love called itself friendship. I called this massive rock home, and though it was cold I would remember summer days when my skin against it had sent warmth to every part of me . . . thoughts to get through an icy winter. "This is love," I would tell myself with each crushing wave. "You pick your stone and you drown with it. If the rock is unmovable, I can maneuver enough for both of us." But when waters rose, when my grip was failing, I would choke and sputter and the rock had begged me, "Don't let go, give me more time," seeing not the peril it placed me in. Only me. Rocks cannot drown. I was panicked and frightened. I wanted still to hold love, hold that rock! But my fingers slipped . . . and I plummeted from the boulder back into the sea. "I'm going under, I'm going to die!" I was shocked, when my feet had touched the earth, to reveal I was only ever waist deep. I was in no peril at all, save for the precarious place I had insisted on clinging to. Now the ocean calls me out to swim. The shore calls me up to dance. So many choices when not bound to stone. I knew a love once that broke me, and it was not love.

Contents

Chapter 1

The Fallout

I used to believe that staying was brave, that no matter how many times I had been broken in this city or this house, to leave would be admitting defeat, running away. I used to believe that not allowing things to change me was courage. Now I think to force things to stay the same, is masochism. I once described myself as not sure-footed. My feet are certain now. I have to go. I don't know what "going" looks like, but having decided this, I'm already partially gone. Once I knew this, now that I know this, it is only a matter of time. What am I doing? Seriously, what am I doing? How do I fix this? How do I fix myself?

People often ask me, "Where did you find the bravery to write your last book?" It wasn't bravery, it was stupidity, and naivety. All I wanted was to write the truth in a way that might make someone else feel less alone. Here's the truth as it stands now: the last book contained lies. Don't get me wrong. I wrote as truthfully as I was able, I wrote things as I saw them, I wrote what I had with the information I had at the time. I assure you though, months later, that book is not what I would write now. I did not have the information I should have been given to write accurately about that time of my life. So here's where truth gets tricky . . . here's the real damage of a lie or lies: they rob us of our narrative. They upset all we knew about the past and alter our perceptions or hopes for the future. They change every memory we had, and now we question . . . **was any of that even real?** I have decided it was very real at the time, but now that I know better . . . it is absolutely not.

My last book began as a novel about a radio host with epilepsy who was being stalked, and it became the true and real-time chronicling of a breakup. This book was going to be another daily chronicling and has instead turned into musings on how I attempt to move on for good. How to force a change. "Start at the end," they'll advise you when setting out to write a book. "Know where the story is going." This isn't a story, this is my life, and I have no idea where it's going.

Chapter 2

January

Jer leans against the hood of his old Beaumont, and I'm perched on a cooler on the floor near his boat. I'm wearing a flannel and boots; he dons a hoodie and socks. How many times have we sat out here in his garage attempting to dissect our problems?

How many times have I walked into his house, tearfully searching for the hug that helps pull the little broken bits of me back together? I was here just last week sobbing in his arms.

"How'd I do this last time?" he joked, resting his head on top of mine. "Let me make this a good one in case you write about it." He turned my sobs into muffled laughter against his chest. "Do I need to tell you to breathe again?"

"I'm just so fucking stupid, I'm such an idiot, what is wrong with me that I . . ."

"Hey." He pushes me away from him to look me in the eyes. "There is nothing wrong with you. I promise." Then he re-wraps me in his hug. Déjà vu, all over again.

"I was out here once by myself . . ." he's telling me now. "And this floor is weirdly slippery in certain socks . . . and I slipped and totally bit it. Thank God no one was around to see it . . . but then, really, I tell everyone about it happening, so . . ."

I've never seen Jer fall over before, and I can't stop laughing at the thought of it.

"Your new nickname can be 'Slippy,'" we laugh, letting the brief levity temporarily whisk us away from our heavy conversation.

"What are you going to do, lady?" His face is serious again. He's referring to a job opportunity I'm in the running for on Vancouver Island. I'm grappling with this because I know I need a change, I'm just not sure how I'll know which change is the right one.

"I don't know . . ."

"You've got to just follow your gut."

"Well, I did that recently, and it ended it utter heartbreak . . . again."

"That wasn't your gut though, that was your heart . . . and your vagina."

I burst out laughing and dribble some of my beer down my face, wiping at my spill and my teary eyes.

"You're right . . . I knew . . . I knew deep down he was going to destroy me again."

"Yup, and that's OK . . . but . . . I just worry by leaving you'll be in the same boat, only you won't have your support system. You'll be sad still, just sad and alone on a fucking island. He calls or he texts, island or no island, that guy's gonna be a bummer wherever you are."

I laugh. "I just . . . I don't think I have the energy for this town anymore. At a certain point fighting through this isn't brave, it's masochism. I can't spend my life here just avoiding people."

"If he is the number one reason you want to leave, that's not a good enough reason, but I'll support you no matter what you choose . . . but I also don't want you to go."

"He is . . . the main reason," I admit. "But there's just been so much stuff in addition to him. Stuff in life, stuff that happened in the farmhouse. Too many memories, and now it's this big pile of pain."

"I know," he nods. "I was looking at pictures the other day from Christmas five years ago, and it was you and me and . . ." He cites his ex-wife, our friends Hendrik and Roxy, and my ex-husband, James. "And I just kept thinking . . . imagine if we played those people a video of what our lives look like now. We wouldn't have even believed it!"

"It's surreal." I agree.

This is surreal, this whole thing. My whole life. Nothing has gone like I thought it would. I am not where I wanted to be, or who I wanted to become. Is anyone? Everyone I know lives a life that has slowly become something they never pictured. You can lament over it, you can cry foul, you can feel sorry for yourself forever, or you can just accept it and try to start again. I thought moving was the thing to do, the way that I save myself from becoming some perpetual victim of circumstance, the way I take control of my story. But could I be wrong?

"I thought leaving was my way of letting go for real. Breaking this insane cycle of misery I've been in for the last year."

"What's the common denominator over the last year though?" Jer asks.

"Him," I say.

"Exactly." He pauses, giving me a look that says everything that needs to be said. "But, again, you have to trust your gut."

I don't know what my gut is telling me. That's the worst part of what all of this has done to me. I was already damaged enough when it comes to trusting other people, but now, I no longer trust myself. I'm thinking this to myself when Jer, still leaning against the car, suddenly slips.

"These damn socks!" he yells, laughing. "I almost went down!" Our laughter bounces back at us off the walls and the floor of the garage, wrapping me up like a warm jacket. God . . . this, I don't want to have to miss out on this.

Chapter 3

Taking Shape

"What doin?" I text Lucy

"Just got home from Girl Guides, getting the kids ready for bed. Come on over!"

"So that's kind of the whole plan . . . so far." I've just finished giving Lucy the rundown on my attempt to force a change. "If I can just get the job stuff to line up, I should probably take off to Vancouver Island."

"What did Jer say when you told him?"

"Similar to you, sad to see me go but understands if I need to leave. Doesn't want me to go, but . . . gets it." We're silent for a moment, and the cold winter air bites at my cheeks. I stare up at the starry sky from her balcony. "I'm just so sick of all the rumors and the talk, and the avoiding of too many people . . . I don't feel free here."

"I understand that . . ." she trails off, knowing all too well what it's like to be a prisoner of your past. To walk each day terrified of running into certain people. To scan a parking lot for a certain car before you go into a store.

"This is going to sound wrong, but . . . you should also consider the fact that pretty much anything terrible that could be said about you . . . it's already been said." We both burst out laughing. "I mean, that's terrible but it's true, right?"

"You're right." I laugh. It falls silent again. Both of us knowing it doesn't matter. Both of us knowing once a Roo has made up her mind about something, she's going to find a way to make it happen. We're both just waiting for decisions to take shape, but we know a change is coming.

"The other thing is," I start, "it's great to stay in a town because of your friends, and I'm so lucky to have all of you, but other people's lives change too. I can't stay here for you guys and then have other people leave. James is gone now, what if Greyson moves, or Jer, or . . . I mean, what if you guys move?"

"We don't have the money to ever move," she replies.

"Well, that's GREAT news," I say sarcastically, and she laughs.

Chapter 4

Checked Out

Nothing is happening. That's the problem with actively deciding you want a change: even when you're trying to force it, it still takes time. I'm too much inside my own head. I am not attached to my body.

I'm in a new class that Hendrik is running. Roxy is in it, and all the other girls are complete badasses. We're talking pro fighters and ju jitsu medal winners. True champions. I struggle to keep up. Every movement is a grind. I'm too inside my head to get this physical, so it's only marginally surprising to me when I fuck up . . . somewhat badly. I'm lying on the ground doing something called a Turkish get-up with a kettlebell. I have completed the movement on one side and now I'm switching sides. All I'm doing is lying splayed on my back while I drag the kettlebell on the floor above my head to my other side. It should remain on the floor while I drag it. Not paying attention, I pull slightly harder than is necessary, causing it to lift off the ground and then striking myself in the forehead with it.

"Kid!" Hendrix yells out.

"Fuck." I place both hands over the spot where I smoked myself. "I don't know what I was thinking. . ."

I'm mortified to have injured myself in such a stupid way in front of all these chicks.

"You OK? Need ice?" Hendrik asks.

"Nah, I'm good." I wave him off, but I'm really not good, I just don't want to make even more of a scene.

Roxy comes up behind me.

"Did you knock some sense into yourself?" she jokes. I laugh.

"Going to take more than that to straighten me out." She smiles back.

I have a meeting with a real estate agent to see what he thinks I could list the farmhouse for. I'll need to sell this one and buy another wherever I land so I can force this change. I never would have thought I'd part with this house, but this is happening. I deserve a chance to start again, and I can't do that here.

The agent is my friend Eli's husband, and he's genuine and kind. I met them through Jer. He seems to understand, probably via his wife and Jer, that this is difficult for me. I'm pleasantly surprised at what he thinks I could list for. This would give me more than enough to turn around and buy another home and still have money left for renovations. Granted, the listing price will likely not be what I receive in the end, but the margins are good.

"This gives you an idea of what you'd have to do to get ready to show it." He slides me over a pamphlet that outlines tips for staging such as decluttering and making sure the light in each fixture is new and working.

"Thanks, I can definitely get started on some of this stuff."

This is really happening. I am going to sell this house and move. Now I just have to figure out where.

Chapter 5

Eclipse

Has anyone else noticed there seems to be a plethora of overly bizarre, dramatically named solar occurrences these last few years? It started with a supermoon, then a blood moon, then a super blood moon, and now today's latest celestial marketing bull-shittery is literally called a "super blood wolf moon eclipse." C'mon, people, the sky and the moon and stars are fascinating enough, you don't have to sell me on it with all these ridiculous names! Still, I don't want to miss it.

I've always loved looking at the stars and the night sky. Meteor showers are my favourite but it's fine by me on any night, let alone when something spectacular is supposed to happen.

As teenagers, Tese and I would watch the Perseids meteor shower every summer in a park by my house. The park wasn't level. The center was this huge basin which made us virtually invisible from the road at this bottom of the field. I'd bring my guitar, she her banjo, we'd smuggle a few beers from God knows where. Lying on the blanket in the center of the park, we'd alternate singing and laughing and drinking.

"Look!" she would excitedly proclaim every time she saw a shooting star. Every time.

"Look, Roo!" Like if I missed a second of it, it wouldn't be as good to her. Like every single one was the most special thing she'd ever seen.

"There is a lunar eclipse tonight. Don't forget to look up." I hit send on the text message.

"Let's go watch it!" comes Greyson's reply.

"Let's take the Beast because 1) Jammer has not much gas. 2) Comfy front bench seat and bring a blanket, park somewhere pretty? Decaf coffee and treats or something?"

"Yup, I'll be ready to rock at 720."

I have an additional motivation for wanting to take The Beast. I'm getting rid of it. Much like my decision to change my life, I'm not sure how or where or when it's going to happen, but it is happening. I have decided, and so it is so. That-mother-fucking-stupid-ass-bane-of-my-existence truck. At one point I thought it was gone, I gave it back, and then it wound up back at my place, and this went on and on and on. Fox would die laughing when she showed up at the farmhouse, and there it was back in the driveway.

"No!" She would point and laugh and cover her eyes empathically. "Again?"

"Yeah . . . again."

"God, it's like a Ouija board, you can't ever get rid of it." We had squealed with laughter.

It's not funny anymore though. The last time she pulled in she stepped out of her vehicle, her body showing me her sadness before she even spoke. She looked at me and just went, "Aw . . . man."

I don't want it. I hate seeing it. I resent that I have been left with the responsibility of dealing with it. The thing is like a fucking Ouija board, I hate the memories it calls forth. I hate the demons it summons inside of me. I want to leave things better than I found them though, I want closure where it's available. I want to overwrite all of the negative with something beautiful. Maybe tonight I can do this with the eclipse, with Greyson, in the beast.

"Treats?" I raise my eyes at Greyson, who's sitting in the driver's seat.

"Much yes." He nods.

In the convenience store we buy a little bit of everything, chocolate, chips, and pop. We drive all through town way across to the other side of the lake and park the truck down near the water looking back towards the moon. I pull the blanket around us, and I lean my head on Greyson's shoulder. We eat our snacks and we joke and laugh. We watch as the moon fully disappears. We wait and wait for it to come back, but it seems to be taking forever.

We google to try and figure out from which direction we think the light will reappear.

"I'm actually getting worried right now," I joke. "What if it's not coming back?"

"I'm feeling very triggered by this," he jokes back.

"I've got post lunar eclipse induced stress."

"I'm offended by the moon's lack of transparency about when it will be returning . . ."

We get each other in stitches laughing. I am so happy in this moment with him. We never stood a chance, yet in every way we have still won, still beaten the odds, by being what we are. The very best of friends.

Chapter 6

Goodbye to The Beast

"It looks exactly the same as when you bought it. What's wrong, don't like it anymore?"

Keep your shit together, Roo. I instantly burst into tears in the middle of the dealership.

"No, there's nothing wrong with it, I love this stupid truck, I love it so much, but I just can't keep it anymore." I explain the entire story to one of the men who originally sold it to us.

". . . and now no one will buy it and I've been showing it for months, and I don't know what else to do, but I just can't . . ." I dissolved into sobs.

"Hey, hey, it's OK. I'll give you five grand and take it back."

"Really?" I'm shocked.

"Throw in a copy of your book and yeah."

He extends his hand for me to shake. I bypass it and hug him.

"Thank you, thank you so much. You have no idea what you've done for me."

I drive home and retrieve the appropriate paperwork as well as a copy of my book.

I sign my half of the papers. I hand him over the keys.

"Do you need a ride somewhere?" he asks me.

"No thanks, I think I'd like to walk."

Just like that, The Beast is gone. With each step, I am lighter, lighter, lighter. Further, further, further. I am not the owner of that truck anymore. I am not that person anymore. I am getting rid of it all. I am forcing a change.

Chapter 7

———◇◆◇———

Believing Again

One of the moments I realize I am kind of fucked up goes like this.

I have been texting with a man who I really like. I originally met him many years ago under completely different circumstances, and then we reconnected recently to discover we are both single. Greyson and I had been at the local dive bar playing pool when he and I caught each other's eye and had enough familiarity to chat briefly. The night took off from there and Greyson and I wound up over at his house with several of his friends. We went well into the night and eventually his sober buddy Rusty offered to drive Greyson and me home. We had kissed goodbye, and not like the brief peck kind of kissing, but the good "I don't want to go" kissing. The kind where Greyson had to keep wandering back inside to tell me to get in the car. He's got hands down the best smile I have ever seen. Ever. He's funny, and silly and smart. He has arms to die for. He's a cop and his name is Christian.

We've been texting the majority of the day and honestly, I'm a little bit flabbergasted to be hearing from him. He is, in my mind, totally out of my league.

His text circles around to mention of a concert tonight.

Aaaaaaand there it is. He must assume I have a hookup for tickets. That's the only reason a guy like this would be interested in me.

I write him back that, yes, I heard that show was in town tonight, but sadly I don't have tickets.

"No, I do, would you like to come with me and some friends?"

"Really? I would love to!"

And that's when I knew that I was messed up.

Why did I believe I wasn't good enough for this person? Why was my initial reaction to assume he was trying to use me for something? I don't have to dig deep to find the answer. I know who taught me I am too much and simultaneously, never enough.

I'm nervous the entire way to meet him. When I pull up to his work he's waiting out front and I'm so jittery I cut a car off in front of me as I turn left into the parking lot. Embarrassing.

As soon as we start talking though it feels easy. His friends are nice and he is . . . what's the word for it . . . attentive. I've never had a man be so attentive! He really listens when I'm answering a question. He pulls out my chair for me to sit, he pushes it in. He stands when I stand. He motions for me to walk through every door or corner ahead of him. He pays for my dinner and declines my offer to split it. At the concert in our seats I put my hand on his knee. He wraps his arm around my shoulder. We sing along and have an awesome time, it's just a great show. On the walk back to the parking lot he keeps his arm around me. When his friends head to their vehicles he offers to walk me to my car. We linger for a tiny bit discussing the Jammer, you don't see too many of them so people are always a little curious about how I like it. I lean in to hug him and thank him,

17

we share a sweet kiss goodnight. He shuts the car door behind me.

I phone Lucy . . .

"Helloooo?" she answers.

"Holy Fuck . . ." I tell her every last detail.

"He . . . came into your life for a very specific reason," she says. "To show you that good ones are out there."

"Right? I forgot . . . Lucy, I legit forgot what it was like to be treated that way. I'm so so so lucky to have had tonight happen. Even if it never pans out, you're totally right. He was just this amazing reminder." And that was all it took. In one date, one night, maybe four hours of interaction, Christian made me want to believe again.

Chapter 8

Jam Jar

Lucy and I lounge on her couch. She sips tea and I'm slamming coffee. Her house has become my second home, I have the door code and I come and go as I please these days. Her kids always bring a sparkle to my day, and so I spend as much time as I can soaking up the family feeling her house gives me. They connect me to something; they give me a place where I belong.

"This job on the island is taking forever to sort out. The longer it drags on, the less sure I'm becoming that it's the right thing. I just keep hoping I'll get the proper offer soon and can kind of follow the money, which is normally so not what I'm about, but it needs to be big enough to justify a move of that nature, giving up all of you guys."

"Yeah, you could just move to my neighborhood."

"True. But I've got to decide what I'm going to do for a living . . . should probably follow where the work is."

"True. But you should also just stay here." She laughs. She's 100 percent kidding, I can tell. I'm certain she will support whatever I do, but she is hoping I won't jump ship. We stay sprawled out on her couch watching trash television after she's put the kids to bed.

"My husband is ridiculous." She laughs and holds her phone to me to display an image. It's a sign he and some buddies have mounted onto the back of another guy's truck. He's working out of town, and apparently they're having a prank night. "Guess they've done a whole bunch of stuff tonight, signs up and things moved around, and they put a jar of jam in one guy's lunchbox."

"A Jar of jam?" I ask.

"Yeah."

We're both silent for a minute, and then I start laughing.

"That's not a prank, that's just like . . . an unexpected item in your lunch."

Lucy starts laughing too.

"You're right, that makes no sense."

The more we think about it the harder we laugh.

When I get home that night I take a photo of a jar of jam inside a lunch box and send it to her. A reply comes instantly.

"Omg, fuck that got me, I feel like I will forever hide jars of jam on you now. I apologize in advance."

"I have your door code now, maybe you'll be the one finding jam," I reply.

"*Quickly rummages through drawers looking for instructions on how to change code* I have a Costco membership, I'm upping the ante, just you wait."

I send her back a reminder of my door code to make it even. Game on.

Chapter 9

February

Today is not my actual birthday, but it is the day when all my friends are going to hit the local dive bar and join me for some food and beers and a few games of pool. I haven't felt this excited about something in quite some time, and poor Greyson must be sick of me saying, "I can't wait until Friday" every day this week. The day is tempered with a bitter sweetness though, as the formal offer from the job on the island has come through. It's financially not where I want it to be . . . yet, but it isn't so far off the mark that I've written it off. What if this is my last night with everybody? What if this is my last birthday I get to spend with them? Lately I'm questioning more and more if this is the right path. I've been paying attention to all the wrong things. How long I lamented "being alone." How much I missed one person. I can't believe I didn't see how much I had. **Have.** Perhaps that's one truly beautiful thing that's come out of my first book. I thought my world was small, I thought I didn't have very many friends. So many people since then though have made comments to the effect that they wish they had the group I do, or they are envious of what strong bonds I have with the people around me. How lucky I am to have these people. I knew, I knew they were all so special, but for some reason in the depths of my sadness I failed to see the fullness they bring to my life. I failed to see that not only are they enough, they're more than enough, they are incredible, and with them I already have so much more than some people will ever have. I'm feeling incredibly sentimental about them today.

Lucy and her kids have made me a cake that the pub said we could bring. Greyson drives her and me down there. Jer and his girlfriend are the first to arrive followed by Hendrik and Roxy, C.J. and her husband, and then Meesh. I'm astounded when each person shows up with a beautifully wrapped present or gift bag. I totally didn't expect anyone to get me anything.

When Hendrik walks in I hug him hard. He knows I'm trying to go. I tell him I got the official offer. We lean over the pool table talking. He's lit in the silhouette of the pub lighting leaning down pensive and listening to me work through why I'm torn on whether I should or shouldn't move away.

"Listen . . ." he tells me. "I'm not employable anymore. After so long working for myself, I don't think I could work for someone else. But it's not easy, your back has to be against the wall, and then you just make it happen. Roxy and I are all about diversification, multiple revenue streams, so one slows down the others pick up the slack. You don't know what you're capable of until your back is against the wall."

"I know. I thought this island job was what I should be doing to get the freshest start possible, but. . ." I motion to everyone else standing around a large bar-height table laughing and smiling and teasing one another. "This seems like a lot to give up. Mind you on the island I could buy a house outright on 7 acres."

"And what," he looks at me with a twinkle in his eyes, "the fuck are you going to do alone on seven acres? Just stand out there with your dogs like, well, here I am."

I burst out laughing.

"If I could combo some writing, some voice-over work, and then maybe just like any old part-time job, maybe I could make it work to stay. Let's face it, I'm qualified for virtually nothing."

He laughs.

"There's lots you're qualified for, just have to get multiple revenue streams going and you'll be set."

We mix back into the group, and I drink, but only reasonable amounts. I'm beyond making myself sick with alcohol these days. Those previous struggles were entirely related to my poor emotional state and low self-confidence. As soon as I extracted myself from that situation my unhealthy relationship with alcohol lifted as if it had never existed. I'm relieved daily by this.

"Let's do gifts!" CJ exclaims, and before I can protest and tell everyone I'll find opening my gifts in front of them all awkward, they're all piling them on the table in front of me. Every single one of my friends bought me a mug, each having chosen one that reminds them of me. Roxy and Hendrix bought me one in the shape of a unicorn. The inside reads "I'm not weird I'm a unicorn!" Jer and his girlfriend got me a Wonder Woman mug and one that says "I can't even . . ." CJ got me one that says "It's not the journey but who you travel with." Meesh purchased me a beautiful flower mug that's totally hippied out. The sentiment and coordination behind all of this is that if I go, I can still have coffee "with" each of them wherever I land. It's deeply moving and I feel a surge of . . . I'm not sure? Frustration maybe? I don't want to give up these beautiful humans to make the changes I need. Am I over-correcting my course and inadvertently setting myself up to crash? Can I make the changes I need without going to an extreme that removes me from the people I love? How do I fix all of this without punishing myself? I know I know I know that I need to make changes, I'm just not certain how far I need to go.

The cake is hilarious and amazing. Lucy's kids went all out on the sprinkles, and it gives me all the warm and fuzzies. The bartender, who Greyson and I know, grabs a microphone. As our favorite waitress carries the cake he trails behind her singing a Louis Armstrong rendition of "Happy Birthday," setting the cake down in front of me.

"Where the fuck did he get a microphone from?" Greyson whispers to me.

"I don't know," I laugh.

Lucy is laughing so hard.

"Cut the cake," she says to me.

I take the large knife to try and make the first cut, but it hits against something and won't go down. I raise my eyes to her quizzically.

"Keep trying," she says to me, dabbing tears at her eyes. I try again but the knife keeps getting stuck.

"It won't go," I tell her.

"Just keep trying." She's laughing so hard and everyone is wondering what's going on, and I'm confused but I keep at it. I manage to work out a piece or two . . . and then I see it. Right in the center of the cake, hidden beneath the icing. A jar of jam. I burst out laughing, and she's crying laughing, and one by one our friends piece together how she's gotten me until there I am, surrounded by everyone I love, uproariously laughing. Perfect. The moment is perfect.

Back at the house Lucy and I sit in my kitchen.

"That . . . was such a great night. Thank you for everything you did to plan it."

"I didn't do much, but you're welcome. Open your gifts from me."

The wrapping paper has sparkles all over it and leaves a trail of fairy dust over my entire kitchen. I carefully unwrap the larger of the two gifts. It's a wooden frame and inside there is a quote that reads "do not go in search of love, go in search of life, and the love you seek shall find you."

The second gift is a tiny package that I unwrap carefully and slowly to reveal an engraved metal keychain. It reads "Do Epic Shit Roo." I throw my arms around her.

"These are so perfect. Thank you so so so much."

When she leaves I am not tired, and I'm not drunk. I sit on my couch. I don't do anything except bask in the glow of all of the love. All of my dumb luck. All the amazing fortune I've had with these people.

Greyson sends me a Facebook message, a video of me cutting the cake.

"Watch Lucy's face when she gets in the frame and you hear the clank of the knife on the Jam Jar."

I watch the video, everyone I love encircling me. Smiling and laughing. Lucy dabbing the tears in her eyes as I keep questioning her, puzzled, and her laughter grows and grows. My heart is too big for my body. The love pours out of my eyes in happy tears.

"So fucking great..." I write him back. "Thanks for an awesome time."

"Pleasure was all mine and the greatness was all you."

"Just crying all the happy tears right now," I tell him.

"Them's the good ones," he writes back.

I knew when I started this I didn't know where I was going to end up. I'm trying to do all this on just a wing and a prayer. It is clear to me now though. I am making the wrong move. I cannot leave these people. I will not leave these people. I have to find a better option. The following morning, I decline the job on Vancouver Island. I have no better prospects, I'm running short on funds and low on hope, and yet I am certain I cannot go.

Chapter 10

The Heads of the Hydra

Jordan B. Peterson is a Canadian clinical psychologist, and his work and writing have massively inspired virtually every facet of my life. I don't agree with everything he says, but many of his teachings have profoundly altered the way I conduct myself. Him and Sam Harris. Game changers. The Hydra is a mythological multi-headed creature, who—when one of its heads is cut off—grows two more in its place. Jordan B. Peterson said, "The problem with lying, is that it's a hydra, and what happens is it has consequences you expect, and maybe you even get away with it. But it has three or four others that you don't expect, and so it grows some complexity. Then you have to tack a lie on each of those little complexity o-crops and then they grow three more complexities, and soon this little lie turns into a great big ball of lies, and at some point the lies becomes painfully evident to everyone."

The Hydra has been chasing me for what feels like a lifetime. I'm tired. Every time I think I have vested it, another head crops up, twisted jaws snarling and snapping at me. They find me on Facebook, they message me on Instagram. They approach me in the grocery store. I cannot escape the heads of this monster. It has caught up with me again the day before my actual birthday. Fuck, this isn't even my monster!!! Why and how does it still come after me? How long will I be punished for believing? I read a book last summer called *Lying* by Sam Harris. I think it should be mandatory reading for every human on the planet. It completely changed the way I conduct myself, and most of my goals now center around living in total truth. It's frustrating, though, when the past isn't in alignment with how I'm setting myself up for the future. Especially when it's out of my control.

In mythology Hercules defeats the Hydra with the help of his nephew, who cauterizes each wound after it's cut so new heads can't grow back, then they burn the body and bury it under a large rock. I feel confident that in burning down my old life, the wake of my flame will catch and kill the monster.

Minutes before midnight ushers in my birthday, the incessant dinging of his texts is the call of the Hydra. Over and over it dings. Drunken and nonsensical. I think of the deep and extreme care I took concerning my interactions with him on his birthday. All that mattered was **his** happiness. These texts are a blatant disregard of what's best for me, directly contradicting what I've told him I need. I've never resented him so deeply. It's never been more painfully evident that my happiness is not of concern to him. The selfishness of this act, it is the final hurtful blow. I do not answer. I cry all night long.

In the morning, my actual my actual birthday is sad and hard. I might not have acknowledged or answered the Hydra but knowing that it lies in wait . . . it hurts me. I was supposed to have dinner with Greyson tonight. I ask if we can rain check.

"No please, don't let this get you down! We can still make the day really special. Why don't I leave work early and come get you?"

"Thanks that's so kind of you . . . I just can't tonight. Another time please."

"OK, let me know if you change your mind."

I spend my birthday in bed staring at the ceiling. For hours.

Shortly before dinner I text Lucy.

"I rain-checked on Greyson. I just can't. Can I come be with you guys tonight?

"Absolutely!" Her reply comes right away. "I'll make you a birthday dinner!"

"Thanks, I'll see you around 6."

Her daughter wishes me happy birthday. "Hey, kid," I say as she walks past me. "I've had a crummy day. What are the odds I can get a hug?"

She flies at me, just flies, and perfectly melts her little body into mine. It isn't a "forced" I-feel-obligated-to-do-this hug, it's a reaching right in and grabbing me by the heart hug. She clings for the longest time and when she finally releases I beam at her and at Lucy.

"Wow! You give the best hugs." She beams back at me.

When the kids are in bed we lie on the couch chatting. I tell her about the messages I ignored last night. She is epically proud. I tell her I've turned the job on Vancouver Island down.

"Best news I've heard all day . . . on both fronts," she says in response. "Still going to move though?"

"Yeah, time to ditch the farmhouse, but let's just find me one around here in a new neighborhood."

"Come be my neighbor!"

"Isn't this the 'bad' part of town?"

"People blow that way out of proportion. It's mostly just families."

"Find me a house in my price range with a suite," I reply.

"On it!" she says, pulling out her phone. Over the next few days she sends me several listings. I reach out to the real estate agent and begin booking viewings.

Chapter 11

Where's Fox?

I open the door and throw her an awkward hug. I haven't seen or spoken to Fox in weeks. A thickness lingers in the air between us. After mounting frustrations with our interactions I had told her I needed space.

"Coffee?" I ask her.

"Yes, please."

Taking her special cactus mug down from the cupboard I pour her a cup and we sit awkwardly at the kitchen bar staring at one another. Neither of us is certain what has caused the rift between us, neither of us likes it, and neither of us knows how to fix it, but we both want to try. So there's nothing we can do other than try, and that's what happens. We sit at the table for over an hour, and tons of tears get shed and voices get raised, and we steer ourselves directly into the awkward and the ugly that we have been avoiding. I tell her things she's done to me that were painful for me, made me feel judged, and have caused my hesitations and concerns with our friendship. She tells me things I've done to her that have hurt her, been incredibly selfish, made her feel expendable, and wounded her on an extremely deep level. It's discomfort. So much discomfort. For long periods of time in between neither of us says anything. It's horrible, the ways we have made each other feel. We're both mad, and sad, and it all around just fucking sucks. There's so much to digest and the conversation at certain points seems to just be going in circles.

"If all the things you think about me are true, then I'm not sure why you'd even want to be my friend anymore," I confess to her.

"That's not fair," she says back. "When you say that it's basically like either, 'Take me exactly as I am and it's your own problem,' or 'Just don't be my friend.'"

She has a valid point on that one. Long ago in our friendship we established a rule that you don't get to argue with how someone feels. You can defend your intentions, or clarify your actions, try and give insight into what you said or how you behaved, but you don't get to disagree with how someone is feeling. It is clear to me I have made her feel terrible. Fucking horrible. Expendable. I hate that. I hate it so much, especially because I'm not sure how to fix it. Especially because when it's been done to me I've asked her, "How could any human be OK with making someone feel that way?" And now somehow I've done it to her. During a long period of silence the ticking of my grandfather clock is the only noise in the house.

"Thought I'd get that up and running again just to really solidify the awkward passing of time during this conversation," I say, motioning to the clock, which has just recently been restarted. She bursts out laughing. I haven't heard her laugh in a long time. There isn't really anywhere huge we can go with this conversation. There's no perfect plan we can form to fix it. That sucks, that's just a terrible feeling. But the trying is all there is in life, is it not? You get the people who hurt you who disappear. You get the people who hurt you who genuinely don't care. You get the people who hurt you who become indignant and defensive by your hurt and refuse to search for their part in it. And very, very rarely, if you're super lucky, you get the people who hurt you, who you've hurt, who will still sit at the table with you. The person who's willing to forgo the awkwardness and the pain and the anger and resentment and simply, and literally, just sit there with it. With you. I see in her how much fight there is left still for our friendship. I see in her that she has faced the darker aspects of who I am, and she still came here today. What is friendship, if not that act?

We resolve to attempt to just restart and tackle certain things as they arise. Neither of us has a better plan than that. We catch up briefly and make small talk about what's new.

When I walk her to the door I hug her long and hard.

"I'm so sorry," I say into her hair and the bunched-up hood of her jacket. "I'll try harder to be better."

"Me too." She hugs me back.

"I love you," I tell her.

"I Love you too." And then she goes.

Chapter 12

Little by Little

It needs some work, but there's something to it. Something that whispers to me, "You're home." This can't be right though. It's the first house I've looked at, literally the very first. The kitchen is far too nice for someone with my meager cooking skills, or lack thereof really. The turquoise walls call Tese to mind and make something inside of me shine. The yard is fully fenced, and I can already see the dogs playing back there. It's six minutes from Lucy's house. This has to be some sort of cognitive bias because I have nothing else to compare it to; it has to be. Who buys the first house they look at? And still . . . I can't stop thinking about it. I decide to put an offer in on it that evening. I go low. The offer is rejected. I feel defeated.

If it's not the Hydra catching up with me, it's my dreams. I do well during the day. I acknowledge the intrusive thoughts and say to myself, "It's not important for me to think about that anymore. This thought doesn't serve me. This thought is not productive." The dreaming me, though, is not so rational. I dream of their laughs. I dream of their voices. I dream of tiny hands holding mine in big parking lots. I am haunted by the living. I dream of being lost in my own house. I dream of not being able to get home. It seems the closer I get to leaving my old life behind the more the nightmares come. I dream of the truth, and I dream of the lies, and I dream I'm trapped not being able to tell which is which. I dream all the things that are real for me when I'm awake, but that I never let myself feel. I mostly don't sleep.

"Nothing else I looked at felt right," I confess to Lucy.

"So offer again on the other one," she encourages me.

We're lying splayed on her couch like always.

"Well, I don't know, I guess I should have gone higher, but there's just things I need to do and I'm not sure how much that will cost. I have to repair some stucco siding and move the stairs in the backyard to make sure the entrance to the tenants suite doesn't collide with my dogs."

"Yeah, but you haven't stopped thinking about it since."

"No, you're right. I haven't. You know what's funny?"

"What?"

"So . . . I've been packing stuff and getting rid of things because I'm determined I'm moving regardless, right, so just trying to cut down and get ready. So I have my mom's wedding dress, and I managed to get it all folded and into this box or whatever. I thought I'd keep it in case through some insane twist of fate I ever get married again. I secretly thought I could sew a tiny bit of material from her dress into mine or something. So I'm talking to her on FaceTime today, and I'm telling her how I got it all packaged. And she starts telling me her concern about my potential inability to utilize the dress . . . which is that it's old and starting to discolour, and for whatever reason I just couldn't stop laughing because I feel like . . . of ALL THE THINGS we have standing in the way of me ever utilizing any part of that dress, the fact that it's discolouring should be the smallest hurdle. I mean, like, it was just this thing where I couldn't stop

35

laughing once I got it in my head, then I got my mom laughing too. I don't have a boyfriend, but . . . the real problem will be down the line when we have to deal with the discolouring."

She's laughing now too.

"I've had a few things like that happen recently," I continue. "Christian and I were talking about crime rates in this area, particularly regarding domestic disputes . . . and I kept thinking, like, well, who the fuck am I having a domestic dispute with? I live alone! And on top of that the realtor when we viewed that house was talking about how the small landing with the up, down, stair option when you first walk in is annoying because 'everyone piles in and there's just no room.' And again all I could think was 'everyone who?' I live fucking aloooooooone."

Lucy's laughing super hard.

"Just everyone worrying about types of problems you clearly don't have, hey?"

"No shit . . . I got my own special set of weird single-person problems, but none of these situations pertain to me."

"Yet . . ." she laughs.

"Exactly . . . yet."

The following morning I offer again on the house. It is accepted. I am moving.

I send Hendrik a text message with a photo of the house and a link to the address of my supposedly rough new neighborhood.

"If your back's gonna be against the wall, may as well pick the hardest fucking wall you can find." I hit send.

"You will be fine." His reply comes right away. "And you're going to love it."

Chapter 13

Valentine's Day

"Happy Valentines day!" The text message from Christian includes a little avatar of him and a card with some hearts.

"Thank you, you as well!" I write back, capping it off with a heart emoji.

We try to coordinate a hangout, but our schedules today just don't line up as I'm busy until the evening and he's on night shift. I'm disappointed because I haven't seen him in a while and I'd really like to. I worry that I did something at the concert that's made him not ask me to hang out again. Whenever those thoughts rush up I just remind myself to be happy that nice guys like him exist and that he showed up to remind me of that. If that's as far as it ever goes, that's still plenty. I keep telling myself that, but I like him, so it's a little challenging.

I train with Hendrik and the girls. I'm still the absolute worst one in the class, which is awesome because it should hopefully mean I'll up my game trying to keep up. In these group classes I get no chat time with Hendrik, which I really miss, but I have the amazing benefit of getting way more Roxy time since she's in the class too. This place keeps me sane and pushing myself.

My training with them reminds me I am powerful. Reminds me to pick up the heavy thing, and put it back down.

I have a contractor coming to the house today. Years ago James and I had a fight, and after I stormed out he put his fist through the shower surround, leaving a gaping hole that remains covered in plastic and taped off years later. STOP! Whatever judgmental thing you are thinking about James, whatever information you think you can infer by the fact that he punched a hole in the shower surround, you're wrong. Dead wrong. Remember that time I tried to smash a microwave with my first? That one off, driven to the brink of insanity, never would normally do anything like that, pinnacle moment of absolute frustration? Yeah, the shower surround was his. He's a gentle giant. Anyways, I never fixed it, and the real estate agent has assured me a potential buyer will try and knock five grand off the house purchase price for something I could repair for like a grand. The contractor agrees and believes he can repanel the surround for about 800 bucks. I FaceTime my parents and tell them.

"Watch out," my mom warns me. "This might be like *Love It or List It*, you'll make all these improvements and then wind up wanting to stay." I laugh because it's clever, but I'm certain that will not happen.

I treat myself to a movie for Valentine's since I don't have a date. It's kind of perfect because *Isn't It Romantic* has come out today and the whole thing is a parody of romantic comedies while still essentially being one. I eat popcorn and treats and sit happily in between two couples. I laugh uproariously at the movie. I give zero fucks what anyone thinks of me.

When I get home Christian and I exchange a few texts. He's having a busy night shift and is hungry. OK . . . I'm going to go for it. I know he likes waffles.

"Well, if you weren't all over the place I'd offer to deliver you some waffles."

"I'm not all over the place."

"Well . . . I'll throw some together then and head your way. Check in with you when I'm in your area."

Fact: You will know if Roo Phelps has a crush on you because she will make you food. I hate making food. I hate cooking. I enjoy baking occasionally when the mood strikes me, but in general the kitchen is the most upsetting place for me to be. So that's how I know, that's how you'll know. Not only do I not mind, I want to. I am excited to make Christian waffles. I even do a very non-Roo-like thing and package it all up as properly as I can in a glass dish with a lid, cutlery, napkins, and little containers with butter and syrup. If this doesn't get me another date with him, I'm at a loss. It's a snowy, miserable drive, but I don't mind. I'm headed out towards what will soon be my new neighborhood, and it gives me a chance to see it at a different time of day. I text him when I arrive outside the dispatch and tell him where he can find me. He parks his cruiser behind me and we step out of our vehicles to meet each other. OH GOD! Seeing him in his uniform takes my minor nerves and excitement and cranks the dial up to 11. My face feels hot and flush, which makes no sense because the air is cold and bitey and around us the snow is falling.

"Hey, you," I say.

"Hi."

"So, you can't judge me on these. I'm not sure how well waffles travel and they're like an hour old by now. Not the finest representation of my skills."

"Oh, I'll be judging you," he jokes. I hand over the bag I've prepared and he places it on the hood of the cruiser. He tucks his hands into his police vest to keep them warm in the cold.

We stand there in the street, the snow falling on us both, just chatting. There's no earth-shattering talk, just pleasant, nice chit chat. He smiles the whole time and it makes me smile too.

"I should get going," I tell him eventually. "I'm sure you don't have a ton of time or whatever."

"OK, thanks for this." He grabs the bag I've made him off the hood. I give him a quick hug and head home. Later he texts to say thank you and tell me they were good. I smile as I fall asleep.

Chapter 14

Trying and Waiting

The day is miserable and cold, and he clutches closed the Cowichan sweater which he wears on top of his dress attire.

"Don't mind the body language. I'm not closed off, I'm just cold."

I laugh.

"That's OK, I get it."

The interview he conducts is quite quick. I used to work for him years and years ago when I was a teenager, but we haven't interacted professionally in at least a decade. I answer his questions honestly, we laugh and joke a bit. It seems to go well. At the end he asks me, "Anything you want to add? Or ask?"

I shift nervously and look at the floor. "I just want to say . . ." I begin, raising my eyes to his. "If you hire me, I won't disappoint you. I promise you I will do whatever you need, and make this a good decision for you. You won't regret it."

"I know, kid. I'll be in touch next week."

He walks me to the elevator and we exchange a hug.

"Thanks again!" I say as the door closes.

"Hello?" comes Greyson's voice on the line.

"Hi! I think I fucking killed it!"

"Really?"

"Yeah . . . I was just like . . . answer everything as best I can, and then at the end I essentially begged, flat out told him, if you hire me I won't disappoint you. I made no efforts to play it cool or anything. I want the job, and I made it super clear. He said he'd let me know next week."

"Awesome. That's so good. Keep me posted if you hear anything sooner."

"I will. I'm headed home now, so I'll let your doggo out. See you back at the house at some point."

"Sounds good."

I drive in silence. I drive in a state of disbelief at my certainty. I drive with one clear thought ringing in my head over and over again.

"I am going back to radio, very very soon."

There's nights and memories and times and days that you recall with an utter sense of dread. There's days you couldn't recall the details of if you were being paid to. There's monumental days like weddings and the birth of a child where your heart swells with joy just recalling them. And then every now and again, there's the type of amazing day or night that happens for absolutely no friggin' reason.

This night starts with Greyson and me playing pool, as many of my best nights have. The vibe, for whatever reason, just feels impenetrably good. Christian shows up with two of his friends who Greyson and I really like, and so the five of us just go . . . and I mean GO! Go like it was the last day of junior high go. Funny side story, his buddy Rusty was the one who drove me home back in January, however somehow in speaking about that night I mention "the cab ride home." Rusty calls me out on it super hard and points out it was him who gave me the ride, we laugh about this tons, but Greyson one ups me. I repeat the story to him about how I foolishly called Rusty a cab driver.

His response . . . "Who's Rusty?"

I die laughing.

"I am!" says Rusty, and then Greyson and I are laughing so hard we can't breathe.

We wind up back at the farmhouse, and everyone enters through Greyson's suite. I frantically run upstairs and tidy quickly, making sure I don't have panties lying around on my bedroom floor for all to see. When I'm finally confident I've hidden any embarrassing items, I make my way downstairs with a 2-6 of gin. The guys are playing Greyson's drums and laughing and joking.

"Do you want to see the rest of the house?" I ask Christian.

"Sure."

I take him upstairs to show him around. When we reach my bedroom I hope maybe he'll kiss me or make a move, but instead we somehow wind up looking at my yearbooks. This is horrifically embarrassing because I was not by any means a cool or attractive teenager. (Damn those girls who are!) We're sitting in my room laughing when the guys yell from downstairs, "Put your clothes on, we're coming up." Christian jokingly undoes his belt to make it look like something was going on. We all laugh and joke with each other, and I honestly could not even tell you what we said or did or talked about, I just remember dancing. Oh my God did we dance! My Marshall speaker never sounded so good, and we crank it as loud as it'll go. And we go until well after 7 a.m.

"I can't find my wallet."

The text from Greyson wakes me up near lunchtime.

"Well...everything hurts and I'm dying, so it seems we all have our problems."

"Can you drive me to go get my vehicle?"

"Yeah, maybe you left it in your car last night?"

"No, I paid at the end of the night, so I obviously left with it. I used cash for the cab. I hope I didn't lose it at the bar."

"I'm sure it's around somewhere, I'll help you look." A few weeks prior to this Greyson and I went super hard and in the morning it was a several hour joint effort to find my keys, so I owe him help on this one.

On the drive to the bar I turn to him.

"You know what, maybe your wallet fell out when you took your pants off."

He looks shocked.

"I took my pants off?"

"Yeah," I'm laughing remembering. "Some song came on or something, I actually can't even remember the context, but I know both you and Christian threw your pants and were just wearing boxers. Sound familiar?"

"Oh right, oh god." He's laughing so hard.

"You guys put them right back on or whatever but it was suuuuuuper funny. I betcha it's in my kitchen somewhere."

44

Back at home we find his wallet right away. It's leaning against the trash can where he flung his pants. What an amazing, ridiculous, random, awesome night.

"Fox!!!!" I yell at the phone screen trying to keep my paint-covered hands off the lenses while I answer her video call. "Hold on, lemme prop this up, I'm painting the dresser." I maneuver the phone to face me while I paint.

"What's going on, how's Costa Rica?"

"It's amazing!"

"How was your friend's wedding?"

"It's tomorrow."

"Oh nice, that'll be good. So tell me what's been going on?"

"Oh my god, Roo, we had the craziest time on the way here."

"What happened?"

"I had a full-on Roo Phelps moment."

"What?"

"Let's just say if I had of had cowboy boots on I would have been cutting them off with a knife."

"Ohhhh no!" I scream at her.

My Nana owned a pair of black leather cowboy boots. Eventually they were passed on to my mom, who then passed them on to me. They were my favourite. They were the reason my ex-husband, James, used to call me Boots. I wore them every day. Every single day.

I wore them the day I signed my divorce papers. I met James at the lawyer's office, we each, teary-eyed, signed the papers, and hugged each other goodbye on the street when it was done. I drove home silently. I didn't call a friend. I didn't listen to music, I just drove. I was blank, and I mistook that for OK. I walked through the front door and slipped my first boot off, but the second one didn't come. The seam on the second one had started to open, and so each pull I gave to remove it from my foot simply expanded the tearing at the seam but did nothing to get the boot any closer to being off my foot. It was very much stuck. I was stuck. And then it happened. The worst panic attack I have ever had. First, I got hot, so hot I felt nauseous, and then I started hyperventilating, and the tears came, and I frantically pulled and pulled at the boot but it wouldn't come. I pulled at the boot as if it were a bear trap and my foot an animal leg. So I lay screaming and crying on the entranceway floor like a toddler in the throws of a tantrum. Eventually I began searching for scissors and in the absence of finding those I pulled a steak knife from the drawer. I cut that boot to pieces. My beloved boot, my nana's boot, my mother's boot. I cut it to shreds with a steak knife.

It was the first time I realized that in the throws of a panic attack I had no ability to think logically or rationally. I could have called a friend to help me get it off. Heck, I could have walked to the neighbors and said, "You're not gonna believe this, but I can't get my darn boot off." I could have asked my tenants. I could have waited until I calmed down and then most likely found a way to get it off myself. I could have calmly looked for scissors and then at least cut along the seams so I would have had a hope in hell of repair later. Nope. In the throes of that moment, the boot needed off now, and it came at the expense of one of the very few material items I treasure that in my right mind I would have fiercely protected. Torn to shreds. With a knife.

"Oh no, oh man . . . what happened?"

"I do not know," Fox says dead serious. "We were getting ready to take off, and it was loud and there were noises and so much motion and I just . . . it just was too much or something. And I started sweating and feeling sick and my heart was racing. There's poor Clive trying to handle me and I've got my head between my knees and he's rubbing my back. Not to mention the other guy in the row with us. I scared the hell out of him. He actually was asking Clive if I was OK. So then the stewardess could sense I was panicking and the more I talked to her the worse it got, and I think she was actually worried I was going to be a real problem or something. So I took my anxiety medication and then I took a Gravol and just passed out. It was so weird. It was the strangest feeling. I couldn't even tell you what caused it."

"Sadly, I totally get it. You're getting weirder, you know," I joke to her.

"I know," she laughs back. "Hey, I've got to get going, but keep me posted on the job stuff, call me or message me as soon as you hear anything."

"I will, it'll be next Thursday, I'm certain of it."

"Right, Thursday then," she smiles. "Bye."

We sign off and I go back to painting my furniture.

Christian and I are seated at the bar of the divey pub we like to play pool at. He's asked about my past, and I'm trying to explain but I'm fumbling a bit, embarrassed. We're sitting so close our knees are touching. I eye my lap when I talk.

"It's really complicated, I just, I made a lot of dumb choices, and trusted the wrong people, and I got burned in a lot of ways by that. I did things I'm not at all proud of, I've made huge . . . massive mistakes, so . . . I'm still paying the price of my own decis--"

"Hey," he touches me softly, raising my chin. "Keep your head up when you talk to me. You have nothing to be embarrassed about." I bring my head up to meet his eyes, which are locked on mine and smiling.

"I was just really dumb," I say into his eyes.

"Naive and dumb are really different," he tells me.

And I've never so much wanted to believe I could be the person I think he sees when he looks at me.

Chapter 15

March

The Thursday I expect to receive the job offer comes and goes. It's Friday now and I've been anxiously checking my phone all day. I've planned a birthday celebration for Lucy this evening, so between the final details of that and packing I manage to keep myself somewhat busy. At 1:32 p.m. my phone finally dings.

I see the manager's name as the sender and the position as the subject line. I pull my phone close to my body, shut my eyes, and repeat one word like a prayer.

"Please, please, please, please . . ."

I open the email cautiously.

". . . it's not you this time, and I'm sorry about that."

The noise I make startles me and the dogs, and before I'm even aware I'm doing it this horrible cry overtakes me. It's a sob, and a wail, and it comes from deep inside my stomach. It comes from inside my heart. This cry punches through the silence of my home and then shatters into a million little soft sobs and hiccups. A million little cries of defeat. A million little sniffles of giving up. It is time I accept it. I don't have any clue what I'm going to do for a living. I have no skills outside of radio.

I Text Jer, "I didn't get the job." He doesn't answer. I don't give him more than five minutes before calling.

HIs voice is cheerful. "Hi, lady, what's up?"

"Did you see my text?" I ask. He can tell right away that something is wrong.

"No? Everything OK, I've got kids in the car, so . . ."

I cut him off.

"I didn't get the job!" I sob into the phone.

"Be there in two seconds."

My front door opens, and he strides in to where I'm leaning against the wall in the hallway crying. He gathers me in his arms.

"I'm sorry," he tells me.

At first I don't say anything; I just cry. I cry because I'm humiliated I can't get a job. I cry because I'm disappointed; I wanted that one so much. I cry because maybe I've made all the wrong choices and should have taken the job on Vancouver Island when I had the chance. When we break our hug I lean back against the wall unable to look him in the eye.

"I was just so certain. I was so certain that I was going to get it."

"Yeah well, you know what . . ." I look up at him.

"What?"

"I was certain my wife loved me," he grins, "and that was wrong, so that's what we do, you and me. Certain of all the wrong things." I burst out laughing. Leave it to him, always, to find a way to make me laugh during these times.

"Listen, it's going to be OK . . ." he tells me. "Two weeks ago that position wasn't even a thing, and you'll find something. Get the move done, get settled in the new place, and we will get it sorted."

"I'm running out of money, Jer," I confide.

"I know," he says. "We will get this sorted. You going to come out on top with some cash after the sale of this house?"

"Yeah, should be some wiggle room, but I have to do some renos at the new place."

"You don't have to do renos."

"No, sorry, not really renos so much as functional changes that I have to do to get the suite downstairs ready to rent. Separate it out more from me and the dogs. I need that sorted so I can have the rental income."

"Right," he agrees. "Makes sense."

"You got kids in the car, right?" I ask.

"Yeah, I can't stay."

"Thanks for coming over."

"Course, go have fun, put this out of your mind for a bit."

"I'll try."

I hug him again and then he goes.

I message the group thread that Lucy, Fox, and I have kept for years.

"Didn't get the job."

My phone rings right away, Fox video-chatting, now in Nicaragua.

"Can't answer," I write her. "Crying too hard and trying to get my shit together to rally tonight for Lucy's birthday."

"I'm so sorry. I wish I was home with you."

The phone rings, and it's my real estate agent. He's had an offer on my house. I should be elated. Regardless of my job situation, this should be a huge burden lifted off of me. I feel nothing. I accept the offer.

I message my parents next. They both have lots of assurances that for now I should just grieve this out and then form my next plan. The offer on the house is great news. It will all be OK. I have only two hours now until I need to get all dressed up and go pick up Lucy.

I curl up into a ball in bed. I pull Atticus close to me and I take his ear, the only part of him that's still "puppy soft," and run it back and forth across my cheek. I find the feeling soothing. Big tears roll down my face and get lost in his fur. He snuggles closer to me, loving me, unconditionally. He doesn't know I'm failing.

An hour and a half later I'm dressed in a sparkly pink bodice, black leather pants, and a sharp little jacket. My makeup is on point. I lean into the mirror.

"Get your shit together, Roo. Tonight is not about you."

The woman staring back at me looks unimpressed. She seems to eye me in a way that says, "I see right through your makeup and clothes. You're not fooling anyone."

"Can I come downstairs for a hug?" I ask Greyson.

"Of course."

I wander through his door.

"Wow!" he smiles at me.

"Right?" I say, striking a pose to show him the outfit.

I hug him long and hard and say over his shoulder, "I can't even about the job. Like actually that phrase . . . I cannot even. Because if I do I'm not going to make it out tonight."

"I know." He squeezes his hug a little tighter.

We chat quickly about the girl he's been seeing and what's new there. We discuss the offer on the house and the implications for his living situation, and then realizing the time I excuse myself to go get Lucy.

Her house is a ruckus of noise and kids and dogs and a husband trying to wrangle all of them while she gets ready. We're out the door shortly after my arrival.

"Coffee first and park somewhere so I can give you your present?"

"You didn't have to get me anything!" she cries.

"Shut up," I respond.

We get our drinks and pull over in a parking spot.

"Here." I hand her a white gift bag from a jewellery store.

"Roo . . ." she says.

"Just open it." She removes the black jewellery box from the gift bag and carefully slides the red ribbon off of the glossy box. Tentatively she opens in. To reveal a tiny Tupperware . . . filled with Jam.

She bursts out laughing and crying, dabbing at her eyes.

"I didn't . . ." she puts her hands over her eyes. "I don't know how I didn't see that coming. Of course the one time I wear makeup I don't wear waterproof." We're both laughing so hard.

"I can't believe you didn't guess I'd do that."

"No, I wasn't even thinking, and the box was so nice I really thought it was . . ."

"Here . . ." I cut her off and hand her a real jewellery box.

"Roo!" she yells again. "You didn't! You shouldn't have."

"I did."

She carefully opens the box to reveal a necklace and a card detailing its meaning. It's a unicorn, and the meaning is all about transforming negative to positive, chasing your dreams, and creating your own reality.

"I love it, thank you so much." She puts it on.

"You're so welcome. Bought myself another one today too, because I'm selfish like that."

"You're far from selfish," she says. "What's it mean?"

"Fire within. It's a phoenix."

"Perfect for you," she says.

"Yeah, except I'm like the phoenix who continually fails to rise. Like a featherless phoenix. I am phoenix failing."

She laughs. She's clasping at the talisman around her neck.

"Everyone has been so nice today. I feel so good!"

"Good," I say.

"What's going on with you and Christian lately?" she asks.

"Equally a phoenix failing to rise scenario. Like, I keep thinking he's going to see me one day and realize how loveable I am."

"You are very loveable," she tells me, "so he's an idiot if he doesn't see that. BUT, the part of you that keeps telling you to wait, that's just your heart-gina talking."

"My what?" I burst out laughing.

"Your heart-gina. You know, like a combo of your heart and vagina."

"No, no, I get it." I'm laughing so hard I can barely talk. "Where do you come up with this stuff."

"Listen, blonde hair and blue eyes, but still," she taps herself on the temple, "very very clever."

"Heart-gina," I repeat back, still laughing. "It's perfect. And what's going on with your 'heart-gina?'" I ask.

"My heart-gina," she laughs, "was put inside a time capsule and buried long, long, long ago, never to be retrieved.

I'm crying laughing. "All right, let's get going."

The night is difficult for me and shatters some of the illusions I've built up about myself. I thought I'd made progress in being social and outgoing, but it's abundantly clear to me now that really I've just been hanging out with the same few people who I'm entirely comfortable with. Put me in a new crowd though and . . . the struggle is real. My genetic condition that causes my poor hearing makes situations like this especially bad. I can't follow what's being said. I don't know Lucy's other friends particularly well, which makes it hard to know how I'm supposed to mix in with them. The background noise in the restaurant drowns out their voices to me. Her friend Lisa keeps asking me if I'm OK, which is super well-intentioned but only serves to further reinforce my knowledge that I appear off. I feel "outside" everything that's happening. It's not for lack of effort on their part. Everyone is nice and attempts to engage me, I just can't get there. They are all drinking, and I want to but I just can't. I've learned enough to know that when my mood is this bad mixing alcohol with it will have dire consequences. Some tiny part of me commends myself for having that level of self-control and care. I also have decided to go ahead with several showings and an open house tomorrow in case for some reason the offer I've accepted falls through, which means I'll need to be up at 6 a.m. to clean and then vacate the house for the day. I can't be hungover tomorrow. The evening is a grind for me, and I make it worse by reminding myself I'm failing Lucy by not being "better" somehow. We hit three different places and just before midnight I excuse myself to go home.

"I love you." I hug Lucy.

"I love you too," she tells me.

I keep it together on the walk through the parking lot, but as soon as I'm in my car, I crumble. The sobs are as loud and as dramatic as ever the whole drive home. Back at the house I eye the case of beer in my fridge. *I could fuck myself right up,* I think. I know that in the mood I'm in, if I'm having one I'm having all twenty-four. Not an option. I snuggle back into bed, where I cry and berate myself. *Why can't you just be better? Why couldn't you have done better tonight for Lucy? Why can't you just be normal? Why is it so hard for you to just belong?*

Chapter 16

Fall Down, Get Back Up

Greyson and I are driving through the mountains, and I'm tearfully telling him how low I'm feeling. We are headed for a snowy winter hike way up high to kill the time we have to be out of the house for showings.

"It's like, I know some of my friends think I should go see a doctor or get medication or something for how dark I get, but that to me is for people who have unhappiness without cause. I KNOW the causes of my unhappiness, and the consequences of my choices, I just can't seem to rectify them. So, like medication won't help me because I'm unhappy for a reason. I just have to fix the reasons."

"Much agreed." He nods. "You could consider more counselling though, that can be really helpful."

"Totally . . . I just know that the job thing, that's what's going to hold a lot of the answers for me. I need a purpose . . . and money."

"Yeah, our father," he jokingly uses our nickname for Jordan B. Peterson, "he says when people come into his clinical practice with depression one of the first things he asks them is about work. It's so important for structure and meaning and everything else."

"One hundred percent . . . I just get so like . . . fuck, I don't want to do my life anymore, and it's not a scary thing anyone needs to worry about, it's just, as far as I can logically see it, the natural reaction to how much my life has sucked sometimes lately. So just gym, and avoid alcohol, and stay the course, and what the fuck else can you do?"

He puts his hand on my shoulder from the passenger seat and just holds it there.

When we step out of the vehicle we wrangle the dogs and I immediately get caught in their leashes. Between that and the deep snow, I trip and fall right down onto my hands and knees. I burst into tears. There I am, incapacitated, like a toddler, sitting in the snow, hands in the air, crying.

"Aww, buddy," he laughs, but it's a kind laugh, and I'm half crying, half laughing, staring up at him from the ground. "Here." He carefully takes my dogs' leashes from me and then removes his gloves and places them over my snow-covered fingers.

"Thank you," I say as he helps me to my feet.

"Any time, Roo."

The ad appears on my screen, and my heart leaps. *THIS HAS TO BE IT.* A local funeral home is looking for a director of family care, and for some reason I am simply certain that this is what I should try for next. I have a real passion for the grieving, which sounds weird, but I just do. Tese's death did that to me. Before she passed away, I'd hear of someone losing someone and I'd utter platitudes about, "Oh, so sorry." Afterwards though, each person who lost someone was me losing her. I felt their loss.

I'd go home and lie in bed and my ex-husband, James, would ask me, "Whatcha thinking?"

"Oh, just about this guy I know at work whose uncle died." Other people's loss would stay with me in a way it never did before. It would register in a way it never used to. Their pain was my pain. I carried them in my thoughts and hearts in a way I did not realize was possible. This is one of the gifts Tese gave me. Losing her made me a deeper and more empathetic person. It made me a person of substance. I am certain that in this role I could help people.

I spend two hours writing a carefully crafted cover letter detailing my experience growing up with a mother who was a coroner, the loss of my best friend, and my general comfort surrounding discussions of death and grieving. I text Christian to tell him that I'm going to apply.

"You would be so good at that!" he replies, which makes me smile.

I send in my application. And now . . . I wait.

I don't feel ready to move. I mean, emotionally I feel more than ready, but having my ducks in a row and the house physically in order and my stuff actually prepared, that's another kettle of fish. Every time I try to pack, this weird sense overcomes me that nothing I own is actually important. I am apathetic about "stuff" at the moment, and my lack of ability to be discerning makes for slow progress. More often than not I lose myself in projects, like painting various items of furniture to match the decor of the new home, versus dealing with my belongings and my current situation. I can only focus on tasks connected to the future, and this house is no longer that. I find myself wandering around in circles staring at what I own with apathy. It's not sadness, it's just a blankness. I really only care about making sure the dogs are OK during the transition and the paperwork and legal end of things has been handled. Still, I half-assedly pack box after box, wondering how I'll feel about what I've brought with me once I reach the other end. The other end. Really only forty minutes away, but a whole other world as far as I'm concerned.

After a brief phone interview the HR firm seems quite pleased with me and books an in-person interview for just two days later. I have to shop. I have no family-care-director-at-a-funeral-home appropriate clothing. I call Jer.

"Sup, brah," I say, affecting a douchey frat-boy tone for no reason when he answers.

"Oh hey, brah!" He kicks it back to me.

"Whatcha doin', man?"

"Oh yeah no, just drivin' . . ."

"Well," I say, changing my tone to my normal voice. "I got a call from the HR firm, and they're bringing me in on Thursday, so I just wanted to tell you."

"Well, well, well," he chides, "it's almost like everything is working out just like I told you it would. It's almost like I told you so, or something to that effect."

"I know, I know. So get this, now I have to go clothing shopping, because I don't have any funeral-home-job-interview-appropriate clothes."

"Yeah, what do you even wear for that?"

"A blouse and a blazer and dress pants."

"Ahhhh," he says playfully "the old blouse and blazer routine." I laugh.

"I'm going to look like a moron. I'll send you pictures when I find something, keep ya posted on how it goes, OK?"

"Please do. And what time do you want me Sunday?" He means for moving day.

"Come by whenever works, I think everyone is showing up around 10 or 11."

"OK, lady, I'll see you then."

In the clothing store I fill an entire cart with items I would never normally wear. I feel that the more unlike me it seems, the more likely it's probably appropriate; however, I'm really shooting in the dark. I ask several women in the change room their opinions and text both Lucy and Fox pictures before settling on an outfit. I send Jer a picture of me in the change room mirror with my new outfit.

"It makes me sad . . ." comes his text. "So it's perfect."

I giggle to myself in the stall.

I'm nervous as I wander down the street towards the office where the interview is being held. My red blazer's collar rubs at the back of my neck in a way that exacerbates my nerves. I hate the idea that this could possibly be the first of many interviews, as the funeral home has sourced out the initial vetting to an HR firm. If it goes well, I imagine I'll still have to interview again with the actual employer.

The interviewer is younger than I would have guessed, and she either likes me, or she's very, very good at faking liking people to get through boring interviews. Possibly a combo of both. There's a bit of joking, and a ton of questions, and the whole thing takes much longer than I thought it would. Most interviews I've done have been really short and sweet; this one drags on for just over an hour. Both the receptionist and the interviewer know who I am from my radio days, and I have no clue if that hurts me or helps me. It's a bit unfair in some ways, really, because even though radio is you being a personality, it's still very much an "affected" version of yourself, like a caricature or something. The larger-than-life version of Roo.

To be judged against that body of work, it's like an actor having to defend their personality based on the actions of a character they played in a film or something. It leaves me feeling misunderstood. She asks about my first book and mentions she'd like to buy it.

"Wanna make your decision about me for this position before you do?" I joke back, but I'm actually not really joking. She laughs.

At home I FaceTime my dad.

"It was so long, Dad. I can't even really describe how it went because it was just . . . a lot. My brain is kind of fried. I hope I get it but I also just am so scared to get my hopes up again like last time because I was so certain." I go over a few of the details that stick out in my head and we chat for a bit.

"Well, sounds like you did all that you could, and now just hurry up and wait."

"Exactly. I'll let you know if I hear anything." A few hours later the HR firm calls and wants to send me a follow-up aptitude test. Some of the questions are ridiculously easy for me, but some of them are so hard I actually have to write a note to the assessor saying I don't have the skills with Excel to complete the task. I feel defeated and I'm worried I've knocked myself out of the running, but I hope that my soft skills and my ability to deal with grieving people will be more of an asset than knowing how to format a spreadsheet. Guess we'll see . . .

Christian has invited me over to his house to hang out, and I'm 10 million times more nervous than I was at the job interview. At least I can wear the clothes I like to his house. The red blazer can stay on a hanger in my closet where no one I care about will ever have to see me in it. His home is beautiful, and he fixes me a drink. I sit at his island and we chat while he makes simple syrup on the stove for the old fashioned he's making for himself. I like that he makes his own simple syrup and drinks old fashioneds. There's something so masculine about everything he does, something that harkens back to an era of "gentlemen" that just doesn't seem to exist in my timeline, or not at least in the men I've spent time with. We only have the one drink, which we savour over several hours of just talking. I tell him all about the interview and the subsequent aptitude test. He talks to me about the books he's reading and lends me one. He knows I strongly dislike guns, so he asks if I want to see the numerous measures he goes to in keeping his safe. After he assures me that learning about them might make me less afraid, I nod and off he goes. He wanders back with a rifle he has retrieved from a locked . . . I make myself laugh while writing this because I was about to say locked locker, and then realized it's more likely than not called a gun locker. He retrieves the rifle from the gun locker.

"Look," he says, laying it down on the island and motioning to two different locks affixed to the gun itself. "This one here is a bolt lock . . ." he explains what it is to me, but the sight of the rifle accelerates my breathing and makes my heart race, so I don't really take it all in.

"And this," he motions to a second lock, "is a trigger lock. That's the scope there . . ." he removes a cap on the end of it. "Hold it and you can look through it."

"Against my shoulder?" I ask.

"Yup, right there."

I place it against my shoulder.

"I shot rifles when I was younger," I tell him. "My mama had my papa's old 22 or whatever, and apparently my nana was quite a shot. Just not a thing for me as I got older."

"I haven't used that one yet," he tells me.

"Where would you, just at the range or something? You don't really hunt, do you?"

"Yeah, at the range, and nah, I haven't had time." He gives me a tour of the house in its entirety and we end up playing darts, which I'm terrible at but love. He's easy to be around and fun to talk to, and he makes the game fun even though he kicks my ass. I can't help but wonder though, just wondering wondering wondering, is this a date? Does he like me? We've kissed a couple times now, and we talk almost every day, but he hasn't made any serious move towards me and he's never really expressed any kind of attraction beyond a friendship. Who knows. I'm happy regardless because he's a fun and kind man, so friends or more, I want him in my life . . . but I don't dwell well in uncertainty. It's reaching the point where soon I'm going to have to ask him for clarification. After several hours and several rounds of darts, we call it. He walks me to my vehicle even though it's only feet from his house. When he lingers near my door to shut it for me, I'm uncertain if I should kiss him or not. I decide if it's going to happen to let him take the lead, and he doesn't.

Chapter 17

Moving

I can't sleep the night before the move, so I load up the Jammer with as many boxes of breakables as I can fit and drive them to the new house. It's exciting using my key for the first time, unlocking the door and wandering up the steps to the living room. This is the first house I have ever bought all alone. I chose it myself and I'll live here by myself. No input from boys. I turn the lights on and just stand there, in the center of the house. It looks beautiful, it smells wonderful, they clearly went to great lengths to clean it. And yet the one clear thought running through my mind is: "What the fuck have I done?"

Have I made a huge mistake? Will this make me miserable? Should I not have done this? Can I be happy here? Will I be lonely here? Will I be OK here? My pulse doesn't race, I have no physical symptoms that accompany the thoughts. This isn't true physiological panic. This is all in my head, and really I suppose maybe the questioning is normal . . . Maybe? I'm not certain. This is only the second house I've ever owned. Here is the thought that I settle on. That I cling to for dear life. That I repeat again and again. I've done some really stupid-ass things and been certain about them, so it logically stands that I could do some smart things and be uncertain. I mumble this to myself over and over like a prayer.

I miss James. Not in the romantic way, but in the way where I know he would encourage me and tell me this is a good house and I chose well.

"Nicely done, Boots," he'd say if he were here. So I shut off the lights and I lock the door, leaving only the exterior light on. I stare at my new front door. And I say it to myself out loud,

"Nicely done, Boots, nicely done."

Moving day is hectic. There were some scheduling problems with the trailer Lucy and her husband are bringing and the timelines for what her husband needs to get done that day. It seems as though they'll need to be loaded up and heading to the new place before I'm able to join them, because I have to be at this house to meet up with the movers who are bringing the giant and more expensive pieces like the fireplace, grandfather clock, armoire, etc. Everything Lucy has coordinated still totally works, but when it comes to important days I get schedule obsessed and I find I'm stressing at the changes. I'm disappointed that I won't actually be at my new place when they arrive with my stuff. I wanted to help unpack and choose where things go; however, I trust Lucy. My phone dings, and it's Jer.

"Just wrapping on breakfast, should the kids and I head over?"

"Yes, please."

When he arrives he can tell I'm all kinds of stressed.

"Hey, one way or another we'll get it done. Kids and I are all yours today, so we got this. Deep breaths, and we'll make it happen." He is always such a calming force in my life.

We take several loads of garbage to the dump before everyone shows up. It feels great to throw away these last reminders of my old life, including my bed and the barbecue. I'm happiest to see them go. Jer jokes with his kids and they giggle from the back seat, which serves as an ailment to the stress I'm feeling. There's no more beautiful sound.

All my friends descend at once, and the front yard becomes a flurry of trailers and cars and SUV's and boxes. It feels like utter chaos to me, but Lucy seems as cool as a cucumber. She has a plan for which stuff to put in which vehicles. She coordinates moving cars to different parking spots and what should go in the trailer. Between her and Jer, it's all under control. *Fuck, I'm so lucky.* When they leave to head to the new place I sit on the deck with Greyson waiting for the movers.

"Man . . . my head's like . . . I'm spun right now. This feels so surreal."

"Normal reaction, I'd say." He smiles at me.

"Right, guess so. I felt myself being snappy, and I totally didn't want to be. I'm not mad at anyone, but my stress is just so high."

"Moving will do that."

"I'm literally going to go lay on the empty floor in the living room until the movers come."

"Sounds good, go decompress."

"Thanks so much for your help. You'll bring my monsters to me later still?" My dogs are locked in his suite away from all the chaos.

"Yup, just tell me when."

"Sweet. Yeah, I just want to get the boxes in and have it be a little calmer before I throw them into the mix. I'll call you later. Thank you."

The movers arrive, and once I've gone over everything with them I head to the new house, where Lucy's husband has ordered pizza for everyone.

"Thanks so much, dude!" I yell to him as he heads out.

When I walk up into the living room I see one of my bras hanging from the fan.

Jer grabs it down, grinning and laughing. His son grabs it from him and runs around with it over his head. "Look Auntie Roo, look Auntie Roo." Lucy is laughing and Jer is laughing, and his kids are laughing, and suddenly the emptiness and uncertainty I felt in this same room last night fades away. People. Love. Friendship. Those are the things that will make me feel I am where I belong. The house is irrelevant. I have not made a mistake.

Lucy and Jer have done a great job of unpacking the necessities and deciding where things should go. Jer heads out to take the kids to their mom's but says he'll be back later. I smooch my niece and nephew and thank them for their help and patience today.

"Oh, man," I tell Lucy. "What a day."

"It went fast," she says. "But you do have way more stuff than I thought."

"I know!" I agree. "No one believed me. Fox is on her way over, and I think we should build my new bed. That's kind of my priority one so I can at least get through the night comfortably."

Years ago, Lucy, Fox, and I sat at the farmhouse trying to assemble a desk and a table. This was back when my hair was coloured a deeply unnatural red.

"Don't you guys feel like we're the setup for a joke right now?" I asked them.

"What do you mean?" asked Fox.

"You know, a blonde, a brunette, and a redhead are trying to assemble a table."

So, naturally, Fox brings this up when we're surrounded by cardboard, Allen keys, and parts.

"Guess since you changed your hair that joke won't work anymore." She motions to my brown-and-blonde highlighted hair.

"Oh don't worry. There will still be a joke in here somewhere, I'm sure."

"Well," Fox announces, puffing herself up proudly with forced over-the-top comical bravado,

"I did assemble a stool from Ikea today, so I'm basically a genius at this. The best part is at home normally I refuse to do anything like that, and so today when I told Clive I was coming over to help you build your bed, he was like, oh-fucking-kay, like who are you."

The three of us laugh.

"It's Saint Patrick's Day," says Lucy.

"I has beer in the fridge."

"I also know for a fact you have green food colouring," she points out.

"Well . . . there's really only one logical option."

We stroll out of the bedroom leaving Fox inside the partially assembled bed frame.

"Guys," she yells, laughing. "A Little help?"

Thank god Fox knows what she's doing, because with her guidance we quickly and easily assemble the frame. I purchased one of those bed-in-a-box things and we gather round in excitement to open it and see what it's like, ohhhing and awwwwwing when it expands on top of the frame. The girls head out, and Greyson and Jer both show up. They each get to work with bags of tools. Greyson hangs my bulletin boards and some of the more essential wall organization items I use for dog collars and jackets. Jer fixes a loose cupboard face directly below the sink. Together they both fix my broken fence panel.

At the end of the evening, when it's just Greyson and me, I feel unsettled by all the change in one day. I crave the familiarity I'm not sure where to find anymore.

"This guy I know is having some drinks with people, it's out by the old house. Want to go?" he asks me.

"Well . . . the problem with that is if I head out that way I'll drink and I won't make it home. I'd have to bring the dogs and everything back to my old house and crash there. It's supposed to be my first night in the new house. It'd be weird if I didn't stay here, right? Convention says I should probably stay here tonight."

"Fuck convention." He grins at me.

"You're right," I laugh. Let's go.

"How was your first night in the new house?" my mother asks me via video chat.

"Well. . ." I laugh. "I stayed at the old house last night! Greyson and I went out for St. Patrick's Day and I didn't want to have to worry about driving and getting home."

"Oh, Roo," she laughs back playfully.

"So we shall see how that goes tonight I guess."

"How is Greyson?" my dad asks, popping into view.

"He's seeing somebody now." I tell them.

"Oh, what's her deal?" my mom asks.

"Haven't met her yet, but if he's spending time with her she must be nice. He says she's like, the kindest person, and that's always most important, right?"

"You're kind," my mom tells me. I snort.

"One, that's debatable, and two, her being kind wasn't an insinuation that I'm not."

"Well, we think Greyson is lovely," she adds.

"I do too . . .long as he's happy, that's most important."

"Have you posted an ad for the suite yet?" Dad asks.

"No, I need to get down there and do some work first. I've got Lucy's carpet cleaner and it needs a whole bunch of little shit and I have to get the fence moved to keep the dogs out of their entrance. I'll do it soon. I just need to settle and form my plan of attack first."

And I do attack the house. Head down, credit card in hand, ever-dwindling budget, I throw myself wholly into attacking what needs to be done.

We met online through a dating site after having chatted for a week or so. Then one day we met in person at a Tim Hortons right by my old house. His pictures were accurate, they looked just like him, but there was a youthfulness to his face that the photos had failed to capture. He is several years my junior though, so it's not an out of place look for him. His name is Thomas, and while I didn't know it when I shook his hand and gave him an awkward hug, I had just met someone who would go on to become super important to me. After hanging out with him twice I was aware enough to realize the romantic spark wasn't there, but there was something about him I absolutely couldn't put my finger on. Something that so deeply intrigued and confused me. He was like this puzzle I wanted to solve. I talked relentlessly to Lucy about wanting to know and understand him. Quiet, somewhat nervous although not unconfident, but he seemed to say so much less than he was thinking. It was easy to spot his high intelligence, discussing literature, abstract concepts and philosophy at length. It was awkward when I'd told him I wanted to just be friends; however, he had navigated it well.

By the time I move into my new place, we're hanging out tons. Bonus, he lives just a few minutes from me now. Hours and hours, kilometers and kilometers of dog walks, have made us close at a rapid pace. Amazing how quickly you can get to know someone when there are no distractions. No booze, no music, no other people, just our footsteps and the dogs, the woods or streets, and our words. He has weird quirks that I adore. He notices things on the street and on the ground when we walk, money, elastics, paperclips, he sees them all. I remark on this and after joking to me that he is like a crow because shiny things catch his eye, the nickname sticks. Crow. It suits him in more than just his pull to shiny objects. It also captures his intelligence and loyalty, so I like that he lets me call him that. He keeps a Ziploc full of all his bread tags, which I like to bug him about. One day he tells me he has also started collecting dryer lint into one bag.

"Dude!" I burst out laughing. "Bread tags is cute, but dryer lint is encroaching on serial killer territory. We need to draw the line."

He laughs back, seeming not to mind my teasing.

"Well, it's because I don't have a garbage can by the dryer, so I keep cleaning it out and putting it in this one bag."

"Yeah, yeah, tell it to the judge."

I share lots of things with Thomas. I wait for him to reveal the source of what I sense is great suffering within him. He does one day, on a walk along a beautiful trail with the sun shining down on us painting an ironically happy backdrop to his story. He has known pain greater than I have. It hurts me to hear his hurt, but in this moment I'm moved that he has entrusted me with it.

"Normally after I tell people there are only two reactions. They either are super weirded out and it's never the same, or they act like it was nothing and we never speak about it again, which doesn't work for me either."

"Well, just so you know, nothing you've told me changes the way I think or feel about you. And it doesn't weird me out at all. I'm more a steer-into-the-discomfort sort of person."

I sense his relief in having told me his truth. I carry it now in a special place in my heart like a small stone. A deep, ugly, dark, but precious black diamond.

Chapter 18

April

The days feel good in the new house. The kitchen has a lot of light, the place feels cozy and homey. Right away I make wonderful memories inside. Lucy and Eli come over for a pizza night. We make homemade dough, and each one of us does up a pizza to our liking. (Both of theirs end up being much more delicious than mine.) The three of us chat and laugh and joke with one another. They tease me about the lack of food in my fridge and the natural desire to want to "mom" me so I can "adult" better.

"I want to take you grocery shopping," Eli laughs.

"Lucy says that all the time too!" I reply.

"Then maybe that should be a hint," quips Lucy.

We lounge on my back deck drinking beers and sharing confidences.

Greyson comes by one evening and as I threw my barbecue out before the move, we decide making burgers on his camp barbecue would be a fun endeavour. Once we're in the store all control goes out the window. We abandon the idea of frozen burgers and opt instead to make the most gourmet, decadent, from-scratch burgers I've ever had. We go nuts on toppings. Tom joins us and the three of us sit on the back deck laughing and telling stories until it's too cold to stay out there. I throw on Counting Crows and kitchen-dance uninhibitedly.

Through Christian, I make friends with a woman named Savannah. She's a police officer too. I liked her so much the night I met her at the concert I went to with him. Now that the moving madness is over, I'm able to get to know her better. She has beautiful thick hair that she's mastered the art of allowing to fall into natural beachy waves. Her eyeliner game is 100 percent on point, those perfect little wings out to the sides. We meet for brunch as our first solo hang.

"Must be weird for you that I know so much more about you than you do about me." She used to listen to me on the radio and she's read my first book.

"I'll just have to catch up to you then." Over coffee and breakfast I instantly decide I want her in the inner circle. In Savannah I find a vault, and while our professions are entirely different, I can tell in some ways she understands better than anyone I've met the struggle between how our careers make the public perceive us, and who we are at our core. I have so rarely or freely implicitly trusted someone. She builds her life around sober activities—dog walks, bike rides, she even invites me to brunch and a craft fair with some of her other friends. Before I met Savannah I'd never gone to a craft fair in my life unless work was paying me to broadcast from it, but with her I enjoy it immensely. I purchase a unicorn horn headband for Lucy's daughter's birthday. We do coffees and texts, and she visits me on her nightshifts when I'm hunkered down at a Tim Hortons writing. I'm excited for Lucy and Eli to have the chance to meet her. I begin planning a housewarming party. I need to get this merry band of misfits together.

"Miiiiiiiiiitch!" I extendedly yell his name when his picture appears on the screen. It's a habit I formed when I was a drunk teenager and now years later, I always say his name like this. The number of voicemails he'd come home to in his apartment in New York after a comedy show that were riddled with me yelling this . . . I can't imagine how ridiculous it must have been.

"You!" he says to me, and I love that he's already laughing. "You better be single right now."

"I am I am, much single. Well, there's someone I like, but . . . who knows."

"No!" He covers his face laughing.

"No, don't worry, it's not like that . . . so it won't be a big deal."

"If he's not into you, he's either blind or dumb. Your affections are always a big deal. Also, stop telling me secrets, because I'm not telling you stuff anymore. No more stuff for you."

"Why?" My eyes grow wide and confused.

"Because . . ." he leans his face down to the camera, "you will tell all my secrets in a book." We both laugh, knowing he's totally kidding. "My daughter was holding your book the other day and she goes, 'She's so pretty!'"

"Awwww!" I scream at him. "That's adorable!"

"And she asked me, 'Did you guys ever used to date?' and I said, 'No, because she's a crazy person, but one time we had a couch sleepover.'" He's referencing a night I stayed on the pullout couch of his hotel room years ago after one of his shows in Vancouver. We'd not slept and laughed the entire night long. "Then she asked me if she could read it, and I told her she's not allowed until she's older."

"Good call. I'm not exactly roll model material."

"You doin' OK?" he asks. Mitch has this sincere way of asking me how I am that I'm never able to evade. It's so genuine, and I always know that no matter how I am, he truly wants to know. That's rarer than you'd think in a human.

"Yeah, I'm honestly all right. Moved into the new place, trying to get a different job, really actually making the changes I need to this time. It's just slow going."

"Good, good for you. Did you paint the entire house blue, or what? I saw a photo and thought you'd gone even more nuts."

"No no," I laugh. "There's a blue accent wall and I did some furniture, but it's not all blue. I promise." I hold the camera up and show him the place.

We catch up on his life, shows he's got coming up, how his daughter is. What his ex-wife has been up to. He's had some medical issues and tells me a horror story about tearing a stitch, describing the scene as "a monster movie! So much blood!" I cover my face and gasp as he describes being awakened by the dog licking his stitches alerting him to the ever-growing pool of blood.

"I go to the ER and the woman told me it was a three-hour wait! I'm holding a towel and bleeding all over myself, so it was faster to actually go half an hour away to the hospital where they did my procedure to have them stich it back up."

"Oh my god, that's just terrible."

"Yeah, and the driver hit every fucking bump on the way."

"Course." We laugh.

He tells me he had a female friend of his borrow the book.

"When she gave it back, she asked if something was wrong with you, so I had to re-read it again, you know, because she thought you were for real a crazy person."

"Why?"

"Oh, just the stuff about throwing yourself off the pier or driving off the ferry. I read it again and it made sense to me just because I know you, you know. So, I told her, admit it, you've thought about it at some point, you just would never ever tell anyone."

"That's true," I say.

"Fuck, when I became a single dad, and I was in Canada struggling to get my residency, I thought I was going to blow my brains out every day."

"Right?" I say.

"So yeah, just funny how someone who didn't know you perceived it, I guess. I didn't read it that way."

"You're OK though now?" I ask him.

"Yeah, no, I'm OK now."

"Good, well I just wanted to check on you."

"Thanks for checking."

"I Love you," I tell him.

"I Love you too."

Christian invites me to the movies with him and his kids to see the new *Captain Marvel*. I have a lovely evening with them, and he walks me to my car and hugs me goodbye after. I shut my phone off during the movie and when I turn it back on, I see repeated alerts from my alarm system notifying me of movement on my front door. I watch a short video clip and spot Lucy laughing to herself. What the hell is she doing? I see it as soon as I pull up to my house. In tiny individual jam packets, she has arranged a pattern across the door. A six-foot-tall dick. She's going to pay for this one.

All week my sweet friends have been sending the same text message. "What can I bring?"

All week my answer has been the same. "Nothing."

I want to spoil the hell out of everyone who got me moved into this house and moved on with my life. I buy every type of booze possible; it's truly sickening the amount of alcohol I bring home, but I want to make sure I have everyone's favourite thing as a thank you for all their help. I buy Costco platters of food and cheese and dessert trays. I buy mix. I clean the house to the best of my abilities. My top standard is probably someone else's daily cleaning regiment, but it looks good in my opinion. I buy a Polaroid camera so my friends can snag pics to take home and leave me with.

Everyone comes. It's the best feeling in the world to have this new house be so full of people, my amazing people! Greyson, Lucy, and her husband. Hendrik and Roxy, Jer, and his girlfriend. Christian and all his friends. C.J., Savannah, Eli, and their husbands. Kristen, Tom, and a mutual friend of mine and Greyson's named Dee. There's about twenty of us, all from completely different walks of life, ages, employment sectors, and incomes. I love it. I love that outside Jer and Hendrik, who are related, you'd be hard to spot a commonality. It behooves one to make friends with the unfamiliar. Although I've told them all not to bring anything, the gifts are mounting in piles all over my kitchen counter. Bottle after bottle of alcohol is added to the already insane selection. Cards and flowers and beautiful tokens of friendship cover every surface. The night starts slowly and then gets rowdier. I never get loser pissed, but I rock a more than solid buzz through most of the evening. Christian, who's just met Jer for the first time, picks him up. Now, Christian is strong as fuck, but he's not the tallest of men, and to see him wandering around carrying Jer's large frame against him . . . ridiculous. They basically play chicken with one another on who is the most uncomfortable with this man-on-man embrace and lift, and to be honest they're both so outgoing and silly that I don't think either of them taps out. It just hits a point where it's unreasonable for Christian to keep carrying him. This leads to more people picking each other up. It gets messier. Tom mingles in and meets all of my friends. Greyson has to open every beer I crack because I've foolishly incapacitated myself with fake nails. Roxy is as bubbly and vivacious as ever. I take a photo of her, Hendrik, Jer, and myself. I don't have any of the four of us together, and I love it. My sweet "family." Greyson takes a photo of himself with the Polaroid, then one of himself holding the Polaroid, and again about four more times until it creates the illusion he goes on forever. A thunderstorm moves in and pelts my house; we crank the music louder in response. My costume jewellery comes out, and Christian's friend Rusty the "cab driver" gets bedazzled up. Somehow, I end up donning my downhill motocross helmet. The only stone-cold-sober person is Christian's friend Len, who's kindly agreed to be the designated driver for his crew. I remind myself I'll have to find a way to make this up to him. I head out onto my deck frequently to smoke, and in one of these brief moments I find myself alone with one of Christian's friends. The chatter is pleasant. He's a kind man and I really like him. During this exchange, though, he makes some comments, so offhanded, so well-intentioned, so lacking in maliciousness, that he has no way of knowing he's said something that's deeply hurt my feelings. It's a simple observation about the type of woman Christian goes for, and the type of woman I am. It's said so nicely, and it is clear this person's preference is me. It's the simplicity of the conversation that does me in. The casualness of what is said indicates to me that this information isn't viewed as any big revelation to anyone other than me. It is simply fact: Women like me, women lacking a certain "Hollywood"-esque quality, do not wind up with men like Christian. Message received.

I crack the bottle of tequila I bought. Then one of Christian's friends points out he's brought me a bottle of coconut tequila, so I should probably crack that too. A group of us do about four shots total within a ten-minute period. The night blurs on into laughing and photos and dancing. People depart one by one, then Tom and Greyson help me tackle the mess. In the end it comes down to 3 a.m. and me and Greyson. We take a polaroid of me leaning over his shoulder, both of us staring deadpan at the camera.

"It looks like an album cover," he says.

"It totally does," I laugh. I crack another beer for me and him, cheers-ing the cans together and pointing dramatically to the sky.

"Straight through till dawn?" I ask him.

"Always," he replies.

Greyson slept in his camper van in the driveway, and I have this plan that I am going to attempt to make breakfast for us before he wakes up. The problem is I'm not sure I even know how to work this oven yet. It works well enough, because within fifteen minutes I've set off the smoke alarm. I do muddle my way through it and manage to cobble together a plate with hash browns, bacon, eggs, and waffles. I knock on Greyson's van door, and his dog barks.

"It's OK, Floof, it's just me," I tell her. "I made breakfast." The hash browns are colder than they should be, and the bacon is over-cooked; however, I nailed the waffles. We sit side by side on my couch devouring every last bite of the greasy food. Greyson heads out. In the afternoon I get an email from the HR firm; the funeral home has decided to go with an internal candidate. It's followed by an email telling me the offer on my old house has fallen through. This is financially becoming extremely precarious and detrimental. I shrug to myself. I am getting very good at losing.

A few days after the party Christian messages me to say hello. I thank him so much for gifts and tell him I was so glad he and his friends were there but explain that I need some space from him for a while. I've realized after my conversation with his friend that I have been fooling myself into believing I stood a chance. I'm certain that if I throw some time at things, I can let those feelings fade and then just be friends. He is respectful and kind and takes it well. I, on the other hand, feel like absolute shit.

Chapter 19

Waitressing

I wander into the restaurant nervously, uncertain whom I'm looking for. I hate moments like this, where it's obvious it's going to be awkward for no reason beyond the simple fact that job interviews are inherently awkward. Are they? Is that a me thing? They never used to be in radio. I'm not even sure what I'll say if she asks me why I think I'm qualified. To be honest, I'm not certain I am. I know I have a track record of staying cool in high-pressure scenarios dealing with the public. I know I'm an extremely hard worker. I know I show up when I'm supposed to and I'm not a complete idiot. What I don't know is if that is enough to make me even a half-decent waitress. I'm not one of those idiots that assumes this is going to be easy. I need this though. I need structure. I need people. I need income while I work on the second book and continue promoting the first. I need to be something, until I'm sure of what I'm becoming. I need this challenge.

We shake hands when she spots me. I like her instantly, and so it pains me when she asks, early into the conversation, that I not write about her. I agree but am already picturing future me holding out pages to her saying, "Just give it a chance and if you hate what I've written I'll toss it out." I think what appeals to me most about her is this: upon first glance I am able to immediately asses that she is a perfect dichotomy. Perfect. She is 50 percent warm and motherly; she has kind eyes and a reassuring tone. Beautiful, and she laughs frequently and smiles often. It's clear she is an incredibly loving person. Then, there's the other 50 percent that just seems to read, as if in capital letters: "DO. NOT. FUCK. WITH. ME." The perfect mama vibe coupled with the ferocity of a mother bear. I love everything about it. It makes her instantly one of my idols. I strive for that balance. Neither side seems to overshadow the other, just a yin and yang. The more she talks, the more I like her. And let's face it: that's rare. More words for me often equals more proof of stupidity, more reason to spot a red flag in another human, more cause for concern or mistrust. Not her. Each thing she says draws me in. I can tell she is a woman with many, many great stories, and I anxiously hope that if she hires me, I will get to hear them.

She agrees to give me a chance. I want to hug her; I want to cry. She has no idea what this means to me, she has no reason to take a chance on me, no clue how much I've struggled, how hard I've faltered to find my footing since choosing to leave radio. Yet for no reason I can pinpoint, it appears she is going to take the chance. That's a weird turn of phrase now that I think of it, to "take" the chance. Because really in "taking" the chance, the only thing I see, the only thing I feel, is her giving. Giving me purpose. Giving me somewhere to be. Giving me something to try at again. Giving me so much more than she is aware of. Of all the moments in time, and people, and places I've been thankful for, it's odd to have one so significant come at the hands of a complete stranger. I hope one day I can tell her what it means. Without a purpose, without a place to be, without a reason to get up, I am nothing. I have been nothing. She has made me a person again. I want more than anything to not let her down. I can tell she is a beautiful, bold, rich character of a human being, but out of huge respect I won't write further of her. It just felt remiss to not give credit where credit was due. God, I hope I don't suck.

So few people call these days, so I'm always slightly and pleasantly surprised when I hear my phone ring. Ah, James.

"Hello?"

"I'm driving home, and nobody wants to talk to me," he says in a feigned over-the-top grumpy little kid voice.

"I want to talk to you!" I yell back into the phone sounding like an excited little kid myself without even intending to. He seems to have a knack for sensing when I need his presence in my life.

"What's going on?" he asks me, and before I've even spoken, I know I'm going to start crying. Someone told me once that you only cry in front of people you feel safe with, and since then I've noticed how with certain people at the drop of a hat it comes out, and with others during times when it would be much more appropriate I've managed to keep it together. My tears are safe with James.

"I just . . . things don't seem to be coming together like I thought they would. I'm struggling with my writing, the job stuff didn't play out how I thought it would. I miss living with Greyson so so so much. I wanted to make this big move and convince myself and everyone else that I could be better, and it's not working, and now I'm embarrassed."

"When do you start the job?"

"The end of this month, but I haven't told anyone that because I'm embarrassed."

"Of being a waitress?"

"No! God no! I'm embarrassed I'll suck at it and get fired after a few shifts or something and then regret having told everyone."

He laughs. "Nah, you'll be good."

I tell him all about how hard giving up day-to-day life with Greyson has been. I tell him about the distance between Fox and me, which I've never been able to fully fix. I tell him about what Christian's friend said to me. I'm crying and blowing my nose while I talk to him, which I do right into the phone and then laugh.

"Sorry," I sniff.

"OK, well, a couple things. You have nothing to be embarrassed about in any capacity and no one to prove anything to, and fuck anyone who tells you otherwise. Secondly, stop always, always thinking it's you. You're just having bad luck and keep meeting shitty confused dudes with bad priorities. You're going to meet a grown-up man one day who knows what he wants, and it will be you."

"I know I don't have anything to prove to anyone. I mean I'm the one who sold them all on the idea this was the best thing for me. I guess I want to prove it to myself? And perhaps some you being right about guys . . . but also . . . a pattern is being established so gotta be a little bit me in that regard. Sometimes I wonder if I am crazy. Like . . . it's been years since I felt stable, you know? Not since we were together, and even then, let's be honest, I wasn't really all that stable either at times."

"You're not crazy, because you're stopping and asking yourself if you are." We laugh.

"Jim Jeffries," he says, citing the name of a comedian we both love. "He says that's the thing with crazy people, they don't know that they're crazy." We laugh again.

"Oh, I'm very much aware I'm not all quite right."

"None of the best people are," he quips back. "Everyone just wants you to be happy. No one is worried about anything other than that."

"I know." We catch up on everything he's been doing. He has lots of entrepreneurial things on the go, some of which include facets near where I live. I offer to do some running around next week that would be helpful to him. In the back of my head I feel like it's the least I can do for all the energy he's constantly expending having to deal with my sad ass. Sad people are exhausting, and on the days when I'm sick of myself and my own story I wonder how he manages to have the tenacity to continue to want to speak to me.

"Wow, yeah, that would be really helpful, Roo. Maybe I will take you up on that."

When we hang up, I feel a little bit lighter, like some of the sad truly came out in the tears.

I was so mad at Seamus that day last summer when we had our spat at the coffee shop, but in the almost year that's followed, we've rebuilt the lines of communication brick by brick. How odd that at one point his idea of me selling the house and starting over offended me so . . . and yet here I am. It seems Seamus saw the path more clearly than I did; however, typical me, I turned away from the trail and bushwhacked my way to the destination. I text him to tell him about my waitressing job.

"Commendable. Think how many people just roll over and fall into depression when they aren't sure what to do. Fuck that. You're pulling yourself up from your boots. That's a hard thing to do. Chin up!"

"Thanks buddy," I write back. "I know I haven't been an easy friend to have this last year, but you were right about lots and lots of things. I see that now, and have been insanely humbled, little by little I'll get there, and I love ya so much."

"It's hard to see the forest through the trees. I get where you were at. I love you too. Never stopped."

I'm not naive enough to have assumed it was going to be easy; however, almost immediately I'm able to assess that it's going to be even harder than I thought. The environment in a restaurant is unlike anything I've ever previously experienced. There are bodies everywhere and you weave and dodge with a constant chorus of "Sorry," "'Scuse me," "Behind", "In front," and "Beside." Every corporate rule I've had rammed down my throat for twenty years about not touching one another or using nicknames goes out the window. The girls hug at the start and end of their shifts, they bump hips, they sneak past, brushing against you. Personal space doesn't exist.

"Behind you, sweet girl," "just beside you, love," "Don't forget the spoon, beauty!" It's surreal to me. There's other terminology that's completely lost on me.

"Eight open all day!" "On the fly!" "Who's expediting?" It's like they're speaking another language. My poor hearing makes this even more problematic, but I do my best just to stay the hell out of the way. If I can't help, my only hope is that I'm not a major hindrance.

The kitchen manager's name is Scott, and during a slower point in one of the shifts he leans through the window and asks me, "So, Roo, where did you come from?"

The question catches me off guard. I'm not really sure how to answer. I'm assuming he means which restaurant, but I clearly have no response for that. So, I smile and reply, "Nowhere."

Kelly is the woman who's been training me. She's petite and cute and super amazing at her job. Not only that, she has the patience of a saint, and trust me, she's needing to use all of it to deal with someone as inexperienced as me. I'm told I'm lucky. Most of my girlfriends have served at one point or another and have prepped me with stories of unsupportive, catty women, tip-stealing, table-snatching, backstabbing. I can tell this place seems different as everyone genuinely wants to see me, and each other, do well. I enjoy Kelly's company immensely, and that makes training extra awesome. She's easy to talk to and fun to be around. Just one of those people with a great energy. I worry every time I mess up. I'm not used to sucking at something . . . not only sucking but, if I'm being honest, being downright horrible. The worst, least-experienced person in the place. This isn't me being hard on myself, this is the truth. What an interesting experience to go from being an expert in your given field, a person whose advice, guidance, opinion, and input were requested and sought after, to being essentially useless. This is humbling. This is difficult. This is all the things I wanted it to be. My ego suffers, oh it hurts, and it aches! It remembers times when I stood on stage in front of crowds of 30,000 people. It remembers times when I won national awards and the esteem of my colleagues. It remembers being the first, or youngest, woman to have accomplished various feats in broadcasting. It cannot, however, seem to remember to place a fucking spoon in a cup of coffee before delivering it to a table.

I like the kitchen manager, Scott; he's got a good vibe. Tall, thin, muscular, and tattooed. We chat occasionally because he's met Lucy in a roundabout way through a charitable organization. I add him on Facebook and send him the odd message. It's mostly just me apologizing for remakes I needed or things I entered wrong. One day when I'm cashing out, we get on about a workout and me tagging along to his gym. He says he'll give them my number for a free week pass. Several days later he messages me to ask when we're lifting and then sarcastically adds the standard weightlifting taunt, "Do you even?"

"When's your gym going to call me about the pass?" I write him back.

"I keep forgetting to leave them your number," he responds.

"Sounds like a you problem," I reply.

We finally get it figured and smash out a leg day together. He's super good company, one of those people that's intelligent enough to discuss primarily concepts, information, and thoughts vs. simply people or events. He's been totally sober for several years, and I find it inspiring. He's also completely done a 180 to every facet of his health after getting sober. Greyson and I have had this conversation many times, about "aiming up," be it in relationships or friendships. In Scott I find an element of that for sure. It's important to surround yourself with people who are improving themselves too. I find him oddly easy to be around for someone I've just met. He knows a lot about things I don't, and so it makes his company both enjoyable and interesting.

On a push day at the gym we're taking turns spotting each other on the bench press. In between, we discuss dating. I can't remember exactly what I said, but he looks at me point blank and tells me, "Too bad we have no chemistry." The comment catches me super off guard for a couple of reasons. One, I wasn't really barking up that tree. I hadn't given any thought to it . . . yet. Two, the outright honesty of the comment truly moves me, albeit somewhat startling and abrupt in nature. We swap positions and I lie down on the bench looking backwards at him.

"So, we have no chemistry?" I ask.

"Nope. Hasn't that ever happened, where you meet someone and think they're awesome but just like, no attraction?"

"Totally," I reply.

I think of Christian. I think of the times I've been crushed by people who wanted to "spare my feelings" by not saying something like this as early as Scott has chosen to. I think of humans who linger in the void of unsaid things simply because the truth makes them uncomfortable. I think of men who convince themselves that withholding a statement like this is an act of kindness, when really, at best, it's an act to avoid discomfort. At worst it's a feeble attempt to obtain the flirtatious attention they might garner from me if they never take this element of the dynamic off the table, even knowing they in no way reciprocate my attraction. I take notice of how easy he made that seem. I honestly cannot pinpoint a single act carried out by a human in the last year that spared more confusion and potential for problems than what Scott's just done. We discuss my philosophies on "truth-ing" at length, and my deep love of Sam Harris.

"It's super cool because once you get good at it, in any situation you never ever have to ask yourself, 'How should I proceed?' or, 'What should I do?' The course of action is always just the truth, so it removes insane amounts of uncertainty, ambiguity, self-doubt. All of it." I talk about Lucy, Greyson, and Jer, our commitment to friendships of this nature. I explain the many ways in which "truth-ing" has changed my life. I can tell he's on board with the idea, and I like knowing there'll be one more truthful spot for me in this world.

Scott and I work out a few times, we walk dogs, we spend an afternoon at the beach. It's during the course of these small interactions that I start to see his sense of humor. Walking back from the sandbar, I'm carrying my shoes in my hand with a backpack over my shoulder, precariously stepping barefoot rock to rock.

"How are you going so fast on these?" Scott calls up to me.

"Dude, I was born on the beach, I'm a natural rock walker."

I look back to where he's fumbling on the sharp stones.

"Well, I must have been born on a meadow then because I'm like Bambi back here." I burst out laughing. He is indeed exhibiting the shaky legs of a new fawn, which is hilarious given his muscular stature. I slip my shoes on at the end of the trail.

"You look like a little kid right now," he tells me. I'm wearing a floral jumper, sockless skate shoes, and, as he points out, my ponytail has fallen to one side. There's no embarrassment, there's no urge to adjust or correct, I simply grin at him like a goof. It's my favorite thing in the world when you find these people that allow you to so uninhibitedly be how and who you are.

"Can I ask you a question?"

"Sure," Scott says to me.

"Agree or disagree. People can change."

"Dude." He laughs, and I love the sound. "Agree 100 percent, I'm living proof that people can change. You wouldn't have even recognized me back when I drank. I am an entirely new person."

"OK, so agree or disagree, 'You can't change people.'"

"Also true. No one could have made me stop drinking until I was ready. You definitely can't change people. Why are you asking?"

"I guess because I want to hear that it is possible to truly change, like, I think I've become someone new, but sometimes parts of your old life keep holding you back, you know? Like it feels like, even though I think my changes are for the better, not everyone sees it that way. I think sometimes people prioritized the wrong things when they looked at my old life, concerts and meetings celebrities and music festivals and everything, but those things weren't making me happy. Then they find out I'm waitressing now and they perceive that as being less of a meaningful life or something, which is so fucked, because so many things about my old life were so fake and just looked good on social media posing with stars. This last year has made me happy, seeing my friends more, and Lucy's kids, and being able to travel and see some of the world. Meet new people." I smile at him. "I know my heart is in radio, but this time . . . sucking at something . . . just sucking so hard at waitressing. There's lessons in all of it and I want to believe that it's truly changed me, because I don't want my life to go back to the shallowness that I believe used to sort of permeate everything I did."

"Then just don't," he says to me. He makes it sound so simple, this man who is walking, living, breathing proof that you can become someone new.

I tell Greyson about him on our next hike.

"So cool," he agrees.

"Right? There's more of us truth-ers out there than we think. It's reassuring."

A week or so later, Scott and I have a random hangout where we get tattoos. Naturally, I select a Sam Harris quote. "Every lie is an assault on the autonomy of those we lie to." And just like that, I have a permanent reminder of a moment with a new friend.

Chapter 20

This Reminds Me Of Something

"Reveal yourself to me!" he screams, waving the can of bear spray in my direction. "I hear you, show yourself!" His face is deep red, and his glassy eyes look right through me. He sweats profusely, his free hand grabbing a hunting knife, then a hammer, then a backpack. He's jittery, erratic, pacey. He picks things up and puts them down. *I am in danger*, I think this over and over again.

"I'm right here, Malcom. It's me, Roo. I'm in front of you," I say to my new tenant, calmly and slowly. I back up in tiny steps hoping my movement won't trigger a reaction.

"I'm going to get them, I'm going to fucking get them!" he screams at the sky, spinning 360 and waving the bear spray can erratically. I don't know if he means me, or my dogs, or some force I cannot see.

"OK," I say. "OK, I hear you."

He disappears inside the basement suite door and seeing my opportunity I turn on my heels running, inside to my suite, to call the police. I get lost in memories, so many memories, of this happening, so many times before.

My high school boyfriend and I lived in a rundown, dilapidated apartment building on a small hill above a strip club. The strip club had carpet table covers and served brunch as a pub on Sundays. All class. I ate there once before realizing there was no way the carpet that covered the tables was removeable to be washed, and that about did me in. Our rent was 275 dollars a month. We had a cat named Bagira who pissed on everything. The neighbors were all drug addicts or dealers. We could have afforded a nicer place but preferred instead to spend our money on Molson cold shots because, and I quote, "They're like alcohol juice boxes!" There were constant domestic disputes. Cars came and went at all hours of the night and day to purchase drugs. No one there was "normal," and I'm ashamed to admit looking back that we fit right in. We used to get wasted every night and play music way too loud, dancing to Billy Joel in the living room well into the early hours of the morning. We threw parties with friends who came for the weekend to visit. We set off smoke alarms from igniting various substances inside, and while I like to think we were somehow less bad than the rest, I'm sure we were rocking that exact same shit rat mentality. The landlord was a pudgy older man with silver hair and a disgustingly high voice. The first time I met him I took one look at him and the words pedophile just rang through my brain. One of those dudes who just made your skin fucking crawl. Not only was he gross and creepy, he was incompetent and so he had hired one of the other tenants to act as the maintenance man. His name was Tony. Tony was in his sixties, and when I first knocked on his door to have my lock repaired, I liked him instantly. He reminded me of one of my elderly neighbors when I was a child. The day he came to repair the lock, I offered him something to drink and was quite surprised when he declined a beer and instead asked if I had tea. We sat drinking Earl Grey for a solid hour, discussing the comings and goings of the building. At the time, I was working the morning show and was always home by early afternoon, so we spent many days like this, him swinging by to fix up the odd thing around my place and me making us tea where we'd then sit and chat. My boyfriend was night shift, so Tony filled my lonely days with wonderful conversation and stories. This went on for several months.

On a particularly beautiful summer day my boyfriend and I, as well as two friends, had spent an entire day at the lake. It was near midnight when we pulled up the steep drive to the apartment complex, where we were met with the blue-and-red lights of two police cruisers.

"What the fuck?" my boyfriend said. "Listen to that."

Blasting louder than you could ever possibly imagine was Patsy Cline's "Crazy."

There were faces in all the windows peering out, but we couldn't see the police themselves or the source of the commotion.

"Get back in your car, he's got an axe," someone yelled from a window.

We shut the car doors and sat watching. The police emerged with Tony, head down, crying, in handcuffs. They placed him in the back of the car and left with him.

The landlord told me later he had attacked another tenant with an axe. I never saw Tony again.

When I lived in the big city, I used to stop at the same Tim Hortons every day on my way to work. All the staff knew me, and I'd linger each day exchanging pleasantries and making small talk. There was a homeless man named Josh who was always seated outside the main doors. I can't recall what our first interaction was or exactly why he and I came to build a rapport. The city had so many homeless it strikes me as odd in retrospect that I developed such a personal relationship with this man in particular. Why did I "see" him more than the others? Had he first started chatting with me, or had I instigated conversation with him? I can't be certain. I do know that at one point it came to my attention that he was simply hungry, and so I began buying him food each day. He liked chicken noodle soup with a white bun, an apple fritter, and a coffee with five sugars. Five sugars! Someone told me people with addictions problems tend to have outrageous sugar orders in their coffees. I don't know if that's true or not. When the days were hot, I'd swap out the coffee for an iced coffee. Some days he was there and some days he wasn't. The odd day if I was running errands and spotted him before my normal departure time, I'd leave early for work so that we could chat.

"I'll be back," I'd say each time I walked past him into the store to get us some food.

"Don't threaten me," he'd joke in reply. My father makes this same joke, and maybe that's part of what I liked about him. He was much younger than my father, probably in his thirties, while I at the time was maybe twenty. I may be misjudging his age though; life had certainly not given him a youthful glow.

"Here ya go, dude." I'd toss him his food and throw my purse down next to him on the pavement. "What's good in the world today?"

Josh always had good and interesting things to tell me. He noticed absurd things people did or said, he'd tell me about adorable dogs he'd seen that day, he'd show me interesting items he'd found on the ground in his wandering. He never seemed intoxicated or high to me, ever. Not once did he behave in a way that gave me cause for concern, although I did worry about him, especially when it got cold or very hot. Eventually we got close enough that our greetings consisted of a hug instead of a hello. One day in summer we sat on the pavement and he was particularly quiet.

"You OK?"

"I'm going to go away for a while," he told me.

"Oh, exciting! Where to?"

"I'm going to go see if I can find my dad."

Josh went on to explain he was adopted but had come into some information regarding his father's whereabouts in the prairies as well as a brother he didn't know he had that he was quite excited and anxious to meet.

"Wonderful, that's so wonderful!" I smacked his shoulder. "I can't wait to hear about it when you're back!"

He seemed sad and scared.

"Hey." I leaned my head against his shoulder. "They're going to love you."

"What if they don't?" He asked me.

"Well, then they're dumb, because MY Josh is amazing, and I have no clue how they wouldn't be able to see that. Hang tight for a sec, K?" I ran back into the store, where I hit the cash machine and returned with several twenties.

"How are you getting there?"

"The bus."

"Well, here." I pushed the twenties against his chest. "For the trip."

He hugged me again and promised he would see me soon.

His absence became a serious point of concern for me. The first week or so I thought nothing of it. By the second week I was curious, and by the third week I was downright worried. Finally I spotted him while I was out grocery shopping.

"Josh! Hey, Josh!" I screamed excitedly, crossing a major street from the grocery store to the coffee shop and narrowly missing being struck by a car. The closer I got the more apparent it became that he did not have good news.

"So?" I asked after hugging him.

"So," he said back.

"Don't want to talk about it?"

"Don't want to talk about it," he agreed.

"Hungry?"

"Starving."

"Be right back."

I grabbed him his usual and though he claimed to be starving he barely touched his food.

"Are you OK?" I asked him eventually.

"They didn't want me then, and they don't want me now."

I don't remember replying. I remember thinking, "Don't say the wrong thing." I remember thinking, "Oh my god what a horrible way to feel." I remember thinking, "I feel bad for telling him they would love him." I remember just thinking so many things, but most of all I remember not having a god damn word to actually say. He deteriorated after that. I saw signs that he was using, and he seemed different but never scary or off-putting to me. He started having "gifts" ready for me when I would arrive. Cool rocks he found, flowers he picked, one time even a pair of shoes. (A law enforcement officer would later point out to me that these were most certainly stolen.) I introduced him to James when we first started dating. Everyone in my life knew that I had a Josh, and that he was weirdly important to me. Then one day he was gone. Unlike the first time, I was worried right away because he hadn't told me of any plans to be away, which seemed unlike him. I asked the ladies behind the counter inside if they had seen him. No one had.

It was exactly three days later when I walked into Tim Hortons filled with disappointment that he was still not there, only to be met with a gaggle of the staff behind the counter pointing to me. Pointing me out to two R.C.M.P. members.

"Have a second?" the kind-faced officer asked me.

"Absolutely."

"Do you know this man?" The officer produced a mugshot, and I was taken aback at the youthfulness of Josh's face in the photo.

"That must be an old picture," I said, eyeing it carefully. "Yes, I know him. Is he OK?"

The officer did not answer my question but instead followed up with, "Last time you saw him?"

"Was three days ago. Is he OK?" I asked again.

"Do you have means of contacting him?"

"No, he doesn't have a phone. Is he OK?"

"We have reason to believe that Joshua"—it threw me to hear his full name—"was involved in a stabbing."

"Oh my god!" I immediately burst into tears. "Who would stab him? Is he all right? Do you know where they took him, or, how did you . . ."

"No." The officer cut me off. "You've misunderstood. This man"—he motioned to the photo again—"is suspected of stabbing someone else."

"Oh." I fell silent. I didn't ask if the other person was OK, because I didn't want to know the answer. "I can't help you. I'm so sorry. I haven't seen him. If I do I'll call you."

The officer gave me a card, which I tucked into my purse.

I phoned James and cried.

"He wouldn't ever have hurt someone unless he had to defend himself."

"I know," James said.

"He wouldn't have hurt me." I'm still not sure If I was trying to convince James or myself.

I never saw Josh again, and he crosses my mind incredibly often. I wonder if he's in prison or still on the street. I wonder if he just left town after whatever happened. I wonder if his dad and his brother ever accepted him. I wonder if he is alive, and if he ever wonders about me. On our wedding day James talked a lot about my relationship with Josh when he gave his speech, and about how my interactions with Josh were part of why he fell in love with me. I love that Josh helped me be loved. I wish I could have done the same for him.

I'm not going to lie. At first, I thought they were a couple. One of the young men was kind-faced and soft-spoken, there was something I initially perceived as being slightly effeminate about him. Malcolm was sterner faced and looked like he'd seen some shit. But he was clear-eyed and smiley, and I liked them both very much. I thought it was cute how the other dude's mom had come with them to look at places. Picking tenants is risky business. I've been a landlord for seven years now and no matter how carefully you try and pick people, you get the odd bad egg. People are experts at deception. I felt good about these two though. New home, new start, new tenants. I knew nobody was going to compare to Greyson, but I liked the idea of having two young men downstairs. They seemed like they'd lend a hand with some of the work around the place, and it felt safe. I hoped to make friends with them, in the pleasant non-invasive "can still respect each other's privacy" type of way. The day they moved in I realized I had misread them, and they were not in fact together; however, it made literally no difference to me.

Each day though seemed to reveal a slightly more . . . oh god, I can't even think of the word. Just a different picture of them, I guess. It happened in extremely tiny increments, so that by the time a month had passed you would not recognize these two boys, Malcolm mostly, as having been the same young men I interviewed for the suite. Knee-length knitted wool jackets exchanged for skull hoodies and bandanas. A tidy haircut replaced with a shaved head. They played their music too loud and had the bass turned up too high, ah whatever. I did the exact same thing at that age. Let the youth enjoy being young. They were always incredibly pleasant and polite to me. Each time I saw them they asked how my day was going or wished me a wonderful night. They often asked me if they were being too loud. They were so considerate. So yes, I was surprised when Malcom got high on meth and triggered my video alarm in the middle of the night by trying my front door handle. Here's how dumb I am: I didn't realize it was him on camera. In fact, I was so worried their suite had been broken into, that at first light I wandered around to the back of the house to make sure they were OK. That's where I ran directly into Malcom, high out of his mind, and waving the bear spray can at me.

Jer is eyeing me in an unusual way.

"OK?" asks Jer.

"Well no, but yeah . . ." I ramble incessantly about the morning and the chaos and the fear and the panic and the police and the sadness. "I think I scared Lucy," I admit.

"You did; she's worried about you. Listen . . . you can't say stuff like that."

"Well, actually I can though." I shrug back.

"I know, but . . .you can't though," he says back. "You have to know that when you're talking like that I have to show up. Because I couldn't live with knowing I didn't do enough."

"You do plenty."

"But if you need more . . ."

"I don't need more!" I protest. "I need to be able to be not OK sometimes, and not have everyone panic. Like . . .sometimes it feels like you all don't understand the difference between someone who wants to kill themselves, and someone who just is overwhelmed with their life. I'm not sure why it's surprising, it shouldn't be new information to anyone that I struggle with not wanting to 'life' . . . but I have been getting up and doing it. I get up and do it. I was just trying to say the feeling is especially hard because the last two days have been so good. I thought the fog was lifting, and now it's just like . . ."

"Like you're drowning, and you come up for air . . . but we don't get that you're still in the water?"

"Exactly."

"I know that feeling. I know what you're going through. But here's the difference, when I had those days, I had two little tiny humans who needed me, and who are going to need me for a long time. So, no other option. And I worry because you don't have that."

"I have those two idiots." I motion to the dogs and he laughs. "Jer . . ." I say cautiously. "I'm really miserable right now."

"Hey." He puts an arm on my shoulder. "I'll keep you miserable for fifty years. So long as I get to keep ya." I tear up. Such kindness. Such constant and unwavering support. "We've both lost enough people, you and me. I can't do it again. So nope, stay miserable, but you're staying." I cry into my hands and lean my head against his shoulder where he's seated next to me on the bar stool.

"I want not to need you guys so much. I'm taking so much more than I ever give, and it's like . . . fucking embarrassing like, here, guys, here's my fresh start, watch this . . . oh wait, I done fucked up again and I have to rally the troops to come and save my pathetic ass because I once again am just . . . failure to . . . life."

"I like helping you, distracts me from my problems." He grins.

We serve the eviction notice, we grab my bikes, we smoke on the deck and chat about other things more lightheartedly. When he goes to leave, we stand at the top of my stairs.

"I feel good now," he tells me. "I was worried on my way over, but I can tell you're OK. I trust you to tell me if you need help."

"I would. I will." We hug long and hard.

"It's gonna be OK," he tells me.

"I know." There's a silence, but we still hug.

He leans down to my ear and in an intentionally comedic, dramatic, over-the-top tone, loudly whispers, "I can't lose you." I laugh and pull away from him, swatting.

"You dork." He grins back at me also laughing.

"Call. I'll be here in twenty if you need me."

"Will do." And Jer walks out the door.

The days that follow are a blur. I deal with the one tenant's mom, I deal with the police, I deal with the residential tenancy branch. I make every move to get them out of my house, but it's a long and slow process. Greyson has been away in Edmonton and we FaceTime occasionally so he can tell me about his trip. I miss living with him so much, and I miss doing my days with him. I head to Vancouver and back for Easter to see my family, and it makes me miss Greyson even more, as he was the last person I went there with. I don't see Jer as often because our houses are so far apart now, but he texts lots to make sure I'm doing OK. On the flip side living so close to Lucy is amazing, we can visit each other with a moment's notice and often do. The landscape of everything I know has become foreign—not bad, just different. That is what I was trying to do, after all, so even when it's uncomfortable there's a strange peace in this. I have new problems, with new tenants, in a new house. That's better than my old bullshit stuff, I guess. I suck at my new job, with new people, and new skills. This is all new. Some days I come home from the restaurant crying, frustrated with myself for not being able to get better as quickly as I'd like. On the occasional day I manage to not entirely botch things, I come home high-flying, waving my tips around to the dogs like I struck it big in Vegas.

Chapter 21

May

I have to get something from the farmhouse, and so I drive by to say hi to Greyson the day he returns from his trip. I hug him long and hard when he walks up the stairs. We sit in my kitchen while he tells me all about his trip. There's no furniture, so he rests perched above the dishwasher leaning up against the fridge and I on the counter resting my shoes against the sink. When he's told me all about his sights and travels, I shift nervously.

"I have to tell you something," I say to him.

"OK."

"I need to apologize to you." He tilts his head at me, confused. "I thought a lot about you while I was away and alone and stuff . . . I've taken you for granted and I want to say I'm sorry for that. I haven't seen the right things, or paid attention to the right things, or however you want to say it. But I see you now, and I'm sorry."

He's quiet for a moment.

"You don't have anything to apologize for, you've never taken advantage of me in any way. You're one of the most appreciative people I know."

"No, not taken advantage of, taken for granted."

"Oh, well, you haven't done that either."

I laugh nervously because I'm certain I have. We chat a bit more and then I head out. On the way home I get a text message from him. It seems he's discovered a problem with the plumbing at the farmhouse. Fuck. I arrive at my new place just as Lucy pulls up to meet me.

"How did it go trying to tell Greyson all your thoughts?"

"Sorry, tonight's a shit show. I just got home and now I have to go back there, something is wrong with the plumbing. And it basically didn't go . . . I pussed out, kind of. I mean I said enough, but it wasn't what I wanted to say or how I wanted to say it. Now I have to go back there to deal with the fucking plumbing. UGHHHHH!"

"I come with?"

"Yes, please."

We drive all the way back to the farmhouse, me ranting the whole time about money and expenses and the mounting pile of bullshit I'm having to deal with between my tenants and now this. I've called a plumber who's supposed to meet us there.

Downstairs we sit at Greyson's table.

"Imagine," I eye them both, "if the plumber who shows up is hot guy from last summer."

"Which hot guy?" they both ask at the same time.

"The one who came and taught me how to solder, 'member? I wrote about him in the first book? The fucking suuuuuuper hot Scottish guy?" The doorbell rings and Greyson wanders off to let the plumber in. It feels like barely a second has passed when he returns and trailing behind him is oh . . . my . . . god.

Lucy sees my panic-stricken face first but can't quite figure out what to attribute it to as he's approaching her from behind. It's him. Hot plumber from last summer.

"Hey!" I stand up and shout out to him. "How've you been?"

"Oh hey!" he grins back. "Great, thanks. How'd your book turn out?" He knew from last summer that I was writing one. Lucy grins, realizing this has to be the same guy I was just talking about.

"Really well, thanks. This is my best friend Lucy and not sure if you remember Greyson." They all take turns shaking hands. My face is 5 million shades of red. He quickly diagnoses the problem as being the water line, which was repaired last summer by the septic company. He had only been here to install a new valve on the water meter. This will be an expensive fix and will require the diggers to tear up the driveway . . . again. I feel like life has come far too full circle. I feel like "The Circle of Life" from *The Lion King* should be playing right now. I feel sick over the money I'm going to have to spend. *Fuck. Fuck. Fuck.*

On the walk back out to the Jammer he trails behind Lucy and me. Hot plumber, whose name is Hayden, mentions he and his girlfriend are no longer together. I want to ask him out, but it seems inappropriate given I'll be retaining his services for this sizeable job. I don't want to make it weird for him if he says no. We all stand around chatting for a brief period and then we each get into our respective vehicles.

"OK, he is soooooooo into you," Lucy exclaims as soon as the Jammer doors close.

"You think?" I ask.

"Ummm . . . yeah! Did you hear how he mentioned which pub he goes to on Wednesdays. Obviously a subtle hint that you need to go there one time."

"I don't know about that," I laugh.

"He's so fucking cute, and super funny."

"Right? He's a really good storyteller. I cannot even fucking believe it was him, that's so weird, like how I said it and then right after he's walking around the corner..."

"Your face was amazing," she laughs.

"Ridiculous," I say in agreement. I fight tears over my financial concerns most of the drive. The waterline means big bucks and having the tenants fail to pay rent and needing to kick them out makes everything a giant fucking mess. Lucy senses my mood is horrible. I feel bad for her because when I get like this there's no pulling me out. I am so fucking broke right now it's not even funny.

"Thanks for coming with me for that," I tell her as we step out of the Jammer and back into my driveway. "Hey look, what's that?" I point to a bundle of tulips someone has left leaning up against my house. I grab at them. "Oh my God, come in. I have to tell you something." I usher her in the front door, where we won't be overhead.

"OK, so yesterday the cute boy-next-door guy was out mowing his lawn, right... and there's all these tulips back there at his house. So we're chatting over the fence and I told him they were my favourite flower. Now look!" I practically jam the bouquet into her face. "Tulips! He left me fucking tulips!"

"Awwwwww ... that's pretty darn cute," she replies.

"Right?! Fucking adorable."

"Ohhhhh, a plumber and a neighbor, well played, Roo." We laugh. Lucy heads out and I fill a vase and place the tulips neatly on the counter next to the ones Christian gave me at the housewarming, which I've kept even though they are dying.

I get asked on many dates and I accept them. I go out with the plumber, with the neighbor, with a childhood friend I reconnected with, really with most gentlemen brave enough to ask. I make it clear to each of them that I am dating other people and that jumping into a relationship is low on my priority list at the moment. I suspect I come off more aloof than I'd like or than I ever was before; however, I refuse to allow any potential relationship to hinder the progress I moved here to make. Spend time together? Great! Go on dates? Awesome. Get to know one another? Absolutely, but I'm not gunning for anything beyond that. I also ditch guy after guy because every date seems to involve them consuming excessive amounts of alcohol, and that's simply not something I want to build a foundation on or invite back into my life on a frequent basis. I have built a little wall around my heart, and it's going to be a long-ass time before anybody gets back in. Besides, finding someone new is not what I'm trying to do right now. Finding myself, fixing myself, re-centering myself . . . that's the end game. I pick up side work writing and creative-consulting to make ends meet. I hustle. I write. I suck at waitressing but try my hardest every second of every shift. I will not allow myself to be derailed again.

Lucy and I sit in lawn chairs at the farmhouse, which still has not sold. Why shouldn't we take advantage of our own private campground? We have a fire going, a few friends around, and she and I have been drinking . . . with ferocity. It is very late. I am loud and drunk and unapologetic. There's no fire ban in effect yet, so Greyson and I have decided this is an ideal opportunity to burn the Christmas trees we have still sitting in the backyard. Yes, I said trees, multiple. We hiked up into the woods to cut a live one down the day after Remembrance Day. Convinced the first would not last until Christmas, I begged him to go adventuring for a second one with me a few weeks later. Now, mid-May, the trees have finally dried and begun to turn brown.

"We so did not need two trees," he tells me, motioning to them.

"Right? Now we know for next year." I laugh.

He burns each tree in several large chunks, which ignite with massive intensity and shoot flames high into the sky, illuminating the entire neighborhood through the darkness. We ohh and awww.

"Speaking of fucking trees, my fruit trees have coddling moth," I say to Lucy. "Which means I either have to pay a shit ton of money to have them treated, or I just gotta take them down. This farmhouse is determined to drain my bank account of every last cent."

Lucy's eyes light up.

"Let's take them down."

"Yes! This an amazing plan, let's fucking chop them down right now!" In retrospect this is one of the more stupid and dangerous things I've done in a very long time. However, at the moment, the plans feels solid.

"Do you have an axe?" I ask Greyson.

"Yeah, but . . ." he motions to it, and we venture off towards the apple tree before he can protest.

"Imma stand way back here . . . just be careful," I warn Lucy as if my words will somehow steady her drunken hands and make this less of a bad idea.

"I got this," she tells me. She winds up and swings with all her might at the tree, the axe bouncing back in recoil, but she controls it and strikes again and again. The sound is deafening and cuts through the rural silence. The apple tree trunk is thick, and she barely makes a dent no matter how many times she swings.

"Girls," comes a voice from behind us, the plumber. "Maybe not the best idea ... one of you is going to get hurt." He takes the axe from Lucy and wanders back to the fire. We follow laughing.

"So loud, Roo," Greyson warns.

"I don't give a fuck," I tell him. "It's my houuuuuse!" I yell loudly. "Neighbors can't evict me!" I scream into the night. Lucy is laughing. We've just gotten reseated around the fire when I remember the peach tree.

"That one should be way easier to chop, it's thinner." Lucy grabs the axe again.

"How are you two the ones that own homes?" Greyson asks us and we laugh.

"Watch this," Lucy tells him as we stomp off towards the back of the property, where the peach tree is. From behind us we hear Greyson narrate to the plumber, "Two landlords walk away ..."

We erupt with laughter.

"You're not going to be able to take it down with that," the plumber calls out after us.

"We really are not very responsible," she says to me when we've reached the tree.

"Fuck," I say, hoisting the axe over my shoulder, "responsibility. For tonight at least."

"For tonight." She taps her beer against mine.

"K, so I'm going to hack off some of the branches rather than go right for the trunk, OK?"

I smash away at the tree, the thudding echoing throughout the neighborhood. We trade off and she hacks off several branches. Exhausted, we still have barely put a dent in what remains.

"That stump is so dead," she says to me, "that I betcha if we just pulled, we could uproot it."

"Great idea," I agree. We set the axe aside and sneak around to the backside of the tree, where we each grab a section of the trunk.

"K, so on three just pull as hard as you can," she tells me. It's so dark and we are so far from the fire that I can't even really see her face, but I can make out her silhouette and feel her beside me equally contorted around the tree.

"OK."

"One . . . two . . . three!" Lucy and I pull and pull and at first there appears to be no give, but then the tree starts to lean. Just when it seems like we might uproot the stump . . . CRACK! The sound is ear-piercing. The tree does not uproot but rather snaps in half and we tumble backwards falling into complete darkness. The pain stabs me everywhere as the entire tree falls onto us.

"Are you OK?" I hear her muffled from beside me under the tree.

"Yeah? Are you?"

"Yeah."

Silence and pain for just two seconds, followed by, oh god, the most uproarious joyous laughter. And the more I hear her laugh, the harder I laugh. The harder I laugh, the more she laughs. Just two best friends, under a peach tree, both bleeding and scraped and cut, laughing like the two of us have not laughed in years.

We have to coordinate getting the tree off of us with as much teamwork as we did pulling it down.

"On three we'll push it off, OK?"

"K," she says.

"One . . . two . . . three." We don't manage to push the tree up all the way, but we do manage to lift a portion of it enough to sneak ourselves out from under it.

"Let's burn it now," I say to her.

"Yes!" Her face lights up in agreement and excitement. We each grab the thickest section we can wrap our hands around and haul the tree up to the fire where the boys are sitting. Their faces are shocked.

"Do not," Lucy says to them, proudly pulling her section of the tree behind her, "tell us that we can't do something."

A full month after I told Christian I needed space, I'm ready to reach back out. I miss speaking with him very much. We also have plans to attend a concert together in the fall, and I want to make sure he knows that I'd still like to do that. The conversation is short and sweet, just long enough for me to thank him for giving me the time and to let him know that I'm good now. It feels strange to hear these words coming out of my mouth. *I'm good now, I'm good now, I'm good now.* I realize I am, for the first time in a very very very long time. *I'm good now.*

"Why are you taking your purse into the bathroom?" Lucy's daughter eyes me suspiciously.

"Sometimes a lady needs her purse in the restroom," I explain. She accepts this answer. Lucy's husband catches my eye as I wander to the restroom but says nothing, obviously assuming I need tampons and not wanting to make a deal out of it. I step inside the bathroom, shut the door, and begin rifling through my purse, but it's not tampons I'm looking for; it's jam. I take out several packets as well as a notepad. Carefully and quietly

I open the cupboards of Lucy's bathroom searching through her things. Bingo! I find it. Her box of tampons. I stuff as many jam packets as I can possibly fit into the box. I carefully place a note on top that reads "Period Jam." I flush the toilet and run the water so no one suspects I've done anything other than use the restroom. It takes all my self-restraint to keep a straight face the rest of the evening.

ding a text from Lucy appears later that night. I open it up to reveal the picture of the jam tampon box and a whole bunch of crying laughing emojis. The text reads, "You mother fucker. I'm dying. I laughed so hard. Still laughing."

Chapter 22

June

I drive home from a coffee with Greyson and am swept up in a wave of deep and profound sadness that settles into my chest and makes it hard to breathe. I'm not crying, I'm just . . . I'm heavy. I miss him so much. I took his friendship for granted so much. I took him for granted. I was so lucky to have this person to share a life and a home with, and now the moments with him feel less intimate and harder to come by. It's not the same, and that scares me. I'm losing my place in his life, and that rips my heart open, leaving it exposed like a raw nerve in a tooth. Everything hurts it when I think of him. And then I am struck with a very clear thought. *Fox.*

I am not mad at Fox. I miss Fox incredible amounts. I love Fox deeply and fiercely. But for reasons I can't quite explain I hit a point in time where I needed to be away from her. I could never expect her to understand, I could never quite get the words right to tell her. My desire to be alone was in no way a correlation to how much I love her. How would you even get that out? "I'm not mad at you, I love you, I just can't be around you right now?" It doesn't even make sense to me. I know how deeply the distance has hurt her, and how the harder we tried to force it, the more damage we did. I think of Greyson, I think of Fox, I think of love. I promise myself I will let go.

The FaceTime song makes my phone sing. I run frantically towards it, not wanting to miss the call.

"Miiiiiiiitch," I yell. "Finally! Sorry we keep missing each other."

"No problem, beauty, how are you?"

"I'm good, I've just been dying to tell you this crazy fucking story. How about you?"

"I have a crazy story for you too!"

"You first."

"OK, so my ex-wife calls me, and she tells me her brother is missing, and she wants me to reach out to some of my cop friends and see if they can figure anything out. I tell her that if she's already called the police there's a process and there really isn't any way any of my buddies can help with that, but I put the call in. Well, eventually it comes out that her brother died at home."

"Oh my god," I gasp. "I'm so sorry to hear that."

"No wait, that's not the story. The story is that the chick who the brother lived with ... she's been in the house, with his body, for like, weeks, Roo. She just kept his body there and didn't tell anybody he was dead." I'm silent for the longest time.

"What? What ... the actual ... fuck? That's like Norman Bates shit!"

"It's crazy." He shrugs. "I'm surrounded by crazy people."

We both laugh even though it's so dark and messed up.

"OK, well mine is less bad than that, but I wanted to tell you about my tenant getting high on meth and losing his shit." I explain the whole story for him.

"Wow. You sure can pick '-em, hey?"

"No doubt, we have both invited some serious crazy into our lives."

"So did you find a new tenant?"

"Yeah, I've got a chick moving in this week, she's quite a bit older than me and it's just her and her cat so should be good."

"It won't be," he jokes, and we both laugh until our sides hurt.

I drive to Christian's house and feel none of the nerves I used to feel in this scenario. The whole dynamic has shifted, I'm just really excited to see him again in person, it's been so long. It's Len's birthday today and a few people are headed out to celebrate, so I've weaseled my way into joining them. The hug I get when I see him feels so good, it's like all the best parts of what made hanging out with him amazing without any of the confusion. Inside he fixes us each a drink and we sit on his couch just talking and talking. I could listen to him talk for days. I don't know if it's the alleviation of the romantic element, the removal of the pressure, or uncertainty, or what, but I find it's one of the best conversations we've ever had. And it doesn't stop. A couple hours later, en route to the pub, I tell him things I've been holding back, things I've been too afraid to say. I see now he is a safe place for me to share anything. At the pub I order coffee while the guys tie it on for Len's birthday. I've only had the one drink a few hours earlier and don't plan on more as I have to drive back to my side of town and work early at the restaurant. The car ride home is hilarious. Len is hammered, so I've agreed to drop him off. What starts off at somewhat coherent directions disintegrates into less and less specifics, until at one point he actually yells to me, "Get in the lane . . . please!" I have no clue what lane he means, and Christian and I are just dying laughing. We get him home safely. I pull up to Christian's house.

"It made me really happy to see you," I tell him.

"Yeah, you too," he tells me back, and I hug him long and hard. On the drive home I think about friendship, and people, and how sometimes things are only painful if we're trying to force them in the wrong direction. An elbow only bends one way. I'm certain any pain I found in my situation with Christian was just that, pushing in the wrong direction, but now I feel we've gotten it right. When I reach my house, I have a beautiful text message from him thanking me for the shared confidences and saying the kindest things about what kind of person he sees me as. I craft him one thanking him for being a man of such profound integrity and telling him I think so much of him. I feel a peace when I think of him now, a peace that I didn't have before. A little safe spot, in a chaotic world.

Lucy and I are pulling out of her driveway to go and run some errands post Monday family night dinner. I shift the Jammer into reverse but as soon as I do the backup sensor trips and beeps maniacally.

"What the hell?" I say. Lucy looks perplexed too. "I gotta get out and check what's back there." I hop out and wander to the back of the Jammer and burst out laughing.

"You bitch!" I scream up to her door, laughing.

"What?" She looks so confused.

"What do you mean, what? You jammed me again."

"I swear I didn't, what is it?" She undoes her seatbelt, racing to the back of the vehicle, where she too can now see it. Jams taped all over the spare tire mounted on the back, jams dangling on strings from the bumper. A giant cardboard sign that reads "Honk if you love jam" as well as a little "#Jamislife."

"You seriously didn't do this?" I ask her.

"No, but look." She motions to the window of her house, where her husband and two kids are peering at us, grinning from ear to ear. Her daughter runs downstairs and out onto the front lawn.

"We got you, we got you!" she yells. All of us stand there laughing. This jam, this hiding of this stupid jam, has become such a fundamentally ridiculous part of what we do and who we are, and it makes no sense, and it's dumb and it's lame, but we have so much fucking fun doing this to each other. When life gets complicated and dark, when times are heavy and hard, we search for answers that are as complicated, dark, heavy, and hard as our problems. Maybe sometimes... just sometimes, we can lessen our burdens with something light and simple and stupid. Something meaningless and nonsensical. Something wholesome, to counteract the vileness and unspeakable unkindness of others. Maybe the joy of life can be found in something as simple as hiding jam.

Jer and I meet for coffee as often as we can, but he's busy with work and kids, and I'm working lots at the restaurant. The moments with him always have one of us rushing off to one place or another, but the confidences shared and laughter is always the same.

"You want a cake pop?" He points to it through the glass of the Starbucks display shelf where we wait in line.

"I want a cake pop, but I'm going to have a protein pack," I tell him, grabbing one and placing it on the counter.

"I got this," he says to me after I place my coffee order.

"I'll also have a large Pike Place roast, and a pink cake pop." He grins at me. "Take your birdseed," he says, passing me my protein pack. I grab it, laughing, and find us seats.

We catch up on our lives, nothing majorly new with either of us, just going over the minutiae of the daily details we haven't exchanged yet. I tell him about Scott and the "no chemistry" comment.

"Interesting," he says, "because at first it sounds kind of mean, but it seems like you didn't take it that way at all?"

"No, I think it was wise of him to say it, a kindness really. I know what you mean though because where Sam Harris is adamant the truth is always the course, Jordan B. Peterson says to 'tell the truth or at least don't lie.' Then there's the idea that honesty without sensitivity is brutality, so I think the situation warranted what Scott said as a pre-emptive measure for any confusion, but not all situations warrant volunteering an unrequested truth. So, for example, if someone says to you, 'have I gained weight?' Sam Harris would argue it does this person no favours to lie to them. BUT . . . to tell a friend out of nowhere they've gained weight could be like, brutality." Jer stares at me long and hard.

"Are you trying to tell me I've gained weight?"

We both laugh, and I swat at him playfully.

"No, you jackwagon."

"Thought maybe you were circling around to something," he teases.

"Listen, I'll be the one gaining weight if you keep feeding me cake pops. Watch, next time you see me my purse will just have all these empty popsicle sticks in it."

"Just pop sticks stuck to your pants," he laughs.

"Do not," I say, waving the empty stick at him, "put it past me."

I know something is wrong instantly. It's not like my father to video-chat me at 6 a.m.

I don't have adequate clothing on to answer the call. From beneath the blankets I pull an arm out to slide the phone to decline, quickly writing a message that I'm just waking up and will call him back in a second. I throw on a T-shirt and PJ pants and wander out to the kitchen island, where I set my phone against my laptop and call him back. He and my mother are sitting side by side on the couch, and it's obvious they've been crying.

"Bert," he calls me by my childhood nickname. "I have some bad news; Jasper isn't doing well."

Our family dog, a beautiful golden retriever. He has cancer and will likely have to be put down. They're waiting on the results of some testing, but it looks very bleak. I keep it together as best I can when I speak with them, but the second their image disappears from my phone, I sob. I text Greyson.

"Jaspy has cancer and will likely have to be put down . . . I has much sad and much tears and much wanting to make the day good for the dogs, would you be up for walking a loop with me?"

"Aw, that's sad. I'm working from home, so yep."

"Awesome, I'll attempt to quit fucking crying and head on over."

I undo the gate and let my monsters into his yard. I knock lightly on his door and he appears. I hug him long and hard and crying.

"Fucking dogs, man," I say.

"Right," he says.

"I just love that damn dog so much, and then I got Atticus when Jasper was only a year old, so it gets me all like panicked about my time with these two." I motion to my dogs, who are now happily playing with his. "Kinda thought maybe just spoiling these guys today would cheer me up. Take them for a hike and then maybe swing by the pet store and get some special treats for them or something."

"Sure."

We walk the same loop we've walked god knows how many times in the last year. Through the forest along a winding path beside a river. Around the back side that overlooks a steep ravine. We journey up a little side trail so I can take a picture of all three monsters attempting to look noble in the forest, along the base of a hill with tall grass and trees and stumps. We take the dogs to the store and buy each of them a peanut-butter bone. Back at the farmhouse we give them the bones and make bets on who'll finish first. Ducky of course practically inhales hers, same with Atticus, while Greyson's dog delicately and gently savours every bite. We're hungry now too so we hit a patio by the water for brunch and linger over food and coffee, catching up. Greyson, as always, has helped make a sad day so much better.

I don't believe I was ever a bad customer; however, waitressing has made me a better one, that's for sure. The things you notice about humanity, people, and relationships when you work at a restaurant, man I could write a whole book on that. There are guests who come in for "the show." They want to be entertained and joked with, they want pleasant chatter and friendly conversation, they want to engage. Did you know I have a superpower? I learned that from an entirely different type of customer. I can become invisible! No seriously, I can stand right in front of someone over and over again during the course of, say, thirty minutes, and a certain type of person will find a way to make no eye contact with me at any point. They can have an entire interaction without ever once acknowledging I am a human. These people act as if your very presence is off-putting. Yet they've come into the establishment with what I assume must be a basic understanding of how the interaction is going to play out, so why are they so bothered that I need to speak with them to be able to serve them? You see the kindest of people when you serve, especially me being so new and so bad and messing up so often. People are patient and more understanding than you give them credit for. They are forgiving with errors and generous with tips. They laugh and diffuse the stress when you're just about to cry. You also see the worst of people. People put off simply by your need to ask them what they'd like to have. People who refuse to answer any follow-up questions like "What type of toast would you like?" or "Do you need cream or sugar for your coffee?" People who basically seem furious that the entire exchange cannot occur telepathically. You also learn people are disgusting—oh god, we're such gross creatures. The amount of times I have gone to clear a plate only to have the person grab their napkin, blow their nose in it, and then place that directly on top of everything for me to carry away. You get good at people-reading. Before they've even been seated you can tell who will be fun to serve and who is going to be dissatisfied no matter what you do. Serving is incredibly entrepreneurial, you hustle hard for those tips, and you can't let up for even a second. Every interaction, every walk-through, every fresh cup of coffee, every item, every exchange, it's all part of the hustle, and each time you err or misstep, you lose money. You fight every second you are on the floor. I am bad at it, but I love, love, love the challenge. Even on days like today, where I'm crying and frustrated and people have been horrible to me, I take an immense sense of pride in the challenge I've laid out for myself. This shift was terrible for me, and I'm so glad it's done. I ring in a to-go food order—our boss generously allows us free meals—and cash myself out. When the takeout box comes up in the window, I see Scott has decorated it for me with "Roobear" written on the top, his new nickname for me. I grab the box without even really saying goodbye to anyone. I just want to curl up on my couch and cry. He calls later to make sure I'm OK. I explain it's just me being generally bad at the job. He offers lots of words of reassurance, which I appreciate. We get cut off on the call, so a text comes after from him explaining he's in Costco and lost service. He ends it with, "Keep your chin up, girl." I am not sure how long I'm going to be serving for. All I know is be it long or short, this experience has taught me so much more than I anticipated, and I've made some friends I plan on keeping for a lifetime.

As soon as the audiologist turns the hearing aid on . . . I can't . . . I can't explain why, but it's like my field of vision has become clearer? It's like my peripheral has opened up and I'm now aware of my left side, which bears the majority of my hearing loss.

"Wow," I say, and I hear my own voice differently. "It feels like I can see better, I know that sounds strange."

"You're not the first one to describe it that way."

I wrap up with them and then drive hell-bent for broke to the farmhouse. I want to hear Greyson's voice. I text him to say I've arrived; he has my dog because I dropped them off before my appointment. I wander down into his suite and he's standing there in the kitchen smiling.

"Hey!" he says. I stare back at him, wide-eyed and grinning like a moron. His voice is so clear, so nice!

"Hi," I say back, still staring in disbelief like an idiot.

"You seem . . . like . . . high or something."

I laugh. "No, it's your voice. I can hear it so well! You have such a nice voice!"

"Oh cool, so you got it then?"

I turn to him and display the tiny device tucked behind my ear. "Yeah, you can't even see it. Cool, hey?"

"So cool! So discreet. So, it makes a big difference?"

"Yeah, but it's weird because . . . like it's so good that it picks up everything, when I touch my hair by my ear . . ." I run my fingers through my hair showing him what I mean. "I can hear my fingers in my hair!"

"Yeah, but if you do that on the other side, can't you hear that? I think you're supposed to hear that." He laughs and then I start laughing, testing what I hear when I run my fingers through my hair on the opposite side.

"Right, that would make sense."

"You want a smoothie?"

"Yes, please." He pulls various items out of the fridge and throws them into the blender. Blueberries, spinach, probiotics.

"This is gonna be loud," he says to me, and when he turns it on it is legitimately the loudest sound I've heard to date. I cover my ears but can't stop laughing.

We sit with our smoothies in the yard talking about books and audio books, our favourite philosophers and authors, and oddly enough the Whim Hoff techniques. (Look it up, it's a whole thing.) He's been busy with his girlfriend and work, he's happy and structured and I'm so proud and happy for him that things are going well. I'm glad to have this catch-up, because he's headed into some crazy busy days with his work. On the drive home I roll the windows down and smile to myself, listening to the wind whistle on the side of my face in a way I've never heard before.

Chapter 23

The Thirsty Marmot

"Whhhhhhhhhy are you baaaaaaarking?!" I scream from under my blankets and the pillow I've pulled over my head. I peek out. Ducky stares at me from beside my bed and gives a single "woof" right at me in response. I look at the clock. 5:50 a.m.

"You're the worst," I tell her, then, "Where's your brother?"

Atticus is barking too from the living room. This is really unusual behavior for these two. What's that sound? Every five seconds or so I hear a . . . chirping? A screeching? A bird? A squirrel? It's like the perfect mix of a bird and a squirrel chattering noise. I open the deck door, where the dogs rush out barking like maniacs at my tenant's car below, which weirdly has the hood propped open on it. I don't allow them to bark at her, or in this case, her vehicle, so I pop them back inside. My tenant appears, frantic and furious.

"There's a marmot in my car!"

"What?" I call down to her. Too early. Brain not brain-ing.

"There's a marmot . . . inside my car. It won't get out."

I've heard of rats and muskrats crawling into engines before, but never a marmot. She must be mistaken; I don't even think a marmot could really fit in between engine components.

"Hold on, I'll be right down." I throw flip flops on and wander around back to her car to take a peek inside the . . . HOLY FUCK! THAT'S A GIANT FUCKING MARMOT!

Peering back up at me with its beaver-esque teeth, the huge marmot chitters and screeches away at me. It's massive, like the size of two cats combined. It's bigger than a jack russell terrier, and it's pancake-d itself right inside the engine.

"Wow, Jesus, he's really in there, hey?"

"Yeah, I've been trying to get him out for an hour."

"What if you poke him with something?"

"I already did." I pick up a piece of baseboard scrap leaning against the house and decide to test the theory myself. I poke him lightly, and his chubby body gives with my nudge but shows no signs of releasing his grip on the spot he's clinging to. He eyes me with annoyance and makes the screechy sound again and again at me.

"Think he's stuck?" I ask her.

"Maybe," she says to me. The dogs are still barking inside.

"Hold on," I tell her. "Got an idea." I run inside and throw Atticus on a leash. I bring him around to her car and let him place his paws up so he can peer into the hood. He spots the marmot and he barks again and again and again. He gnashes his teeth and barks with all his might. The marmot turns his head to one side as if to say, 'you are loud and bothering me, I do not invite this type of noise in my residency.' *Saucy little fucker.* He does not loosen his grip on the engine. I bring the dog back inside and call the conservation officer's line.

"Who do I speak to about this, a mechanic or pest control? I don't want him hurt, but he can't live in her engine."

"Before you call a pest control company, get a hose and just spray him, lots of times water will do the trick."

"Perfect, thank you." I march back outside and unroll the hose. It doesn't have a spray nozzle on it, but I turn the pressure up to full blast. Carefully reaching over top of the engine, I position the hose as close as I can get to the marmot's face. This is definitely going to do the trick. *Eviction notice, bitch. Get out.* I get the hose right in front of him and hit him with it, full force water spraying right in his little face. And then that mother fucker opens his little marmot mouth and guzzles the water like he hasn't had a drink in three days. He loves it! He loves every second of it! He is in marmot heaven! Thrilled with me, he seems to say, "Goodness, how kind, I've been so very thirsty in here." No matter how close I get the hose to him he just opens his mouth wider and takes it all in, lapping it up. Living his best marmot life. I shut the hose off in disbelief. I go inside and call the conservation officer back. He laughs at my story.

"You need a nozzle on the hose to get the pressure higher."

"I don't want to hurt him," I say.

"Trust me, you won't." Time to call in the reinforcements. I need the boy next door.

"Morning, sorry for texting so early, do you have a hose nozzle? My tenant has a marmot in her car."

"Yup, come on over," he writes back. He's pulling jeans on up over his boxers when I walk into his house, and he looks really fucking cute having just woken up. My heart skips a couple beats, for sure.

"Always something with you, hey?" He laughs.

"I did warn you," I tell him. When we first started texting, I warned him repeatedly I'm a shit magnet, and my scales rarely stay balanced for long. I even went so far as to say, and I quote, "you've officially been advised of this and proceed to know me at your own risk." He has remained unprecedently unphased by the oddities life throws at me. He gives me the hose nozzle and follows me outside.

"I'm coming with you," he says. "I gotta see this."

I suspect that like I did, he is questioning if it even is a marmot in the engine. Sure enough, when he leans over to look, he's caught off guard.

"Holy fuck."

"I know, right? It's huge."

"Shoulda worn steel toes," he jokes.

"OK, so I'm gonna spray him just like, as hard as is possible, and hopefully he just drops out. Tell me if you see him under the car." I attach the nozzle and lean right into the engine. I feel bad, but I spray him right in the face. He turns his cheek and almost leans his body defiantly into the water. I do not relent. This is war.

"He's coming down a bit, keep spraying . . ." the boy next door tells me, and then finally, "he's out." I let up on the trigger of the nozzle and turn back proudly.

"He hopped right back in as soon as the water went off."

"Fuck," we both laugh. My tenant is outside now watching this too.

"OK, so this time," I tell him, "take this"—I hand him the piece of trim—"and when he drops down hit him with it from under the car."

"I don't want to hit him," he tells me.

"Well, like, shoo him or whatever." We're all laughing. I relentlessly spray the marmot in the face again, and the boy next door yells, "He's out," and then, "He's gone." But the marmot, having lost the battle, refuses to give up the war. He scurries directly up the back wheel well into the back half of the car.

"Well," I tell my tenant, "he ain't in the engine anymore."

Later that night the boy next door and I are cuddled up on his couch watching *Game of Thrones*.

"Can you pause it for a sec?" I say, walking away from the couch to the kitchen. "I'm just going to get some water." I wander into the kitchen and fill up a cup. I slam a full glass and then refill the cup. He says something I don't quite catch, and I can tell it was cheeky because he's grinning and laughing.

"What did you say to me?" I ask, eyeing his smirk as I cuddle back into his arms.

"I said, 'You're a thirsty little marmot.'" And we laugh. In this moment, I'm stupidly happy.

Lucy and I hang out in her kitchen cooking dinner. Well, really, she cooks dinner while I natter away incessantly. I seat myself above the cutlery drawer on her counter and so every few minutes she has to say, "Spoon" or "Knife," and I'll raise my feet up so she can grab a utensil. My weekly Monday dinners with her family have been going on strong almost a year now, and it's always a part of the week I treasure. Her husband walks in the door from work.

"Hey," I holler down the stairs to the front door, and then as he makes his way up, "have I got a story for you." I regale him with my thirsty marmot story.

The dinner is delicious, and afterwards the kids line up all the lawn chairs to make a train, providing all the adults with their "ticket." No sooner are we seated by the "conductor," Lucy's son, than the kids lose interest and want to play on the swing set. Lucy and I lounge together on a giant saucer swing, her daughter and son crawling on and off of us. Out of nowhere her daughter abruptly smacks Lucy's face.

"Mosquito," she says, and neither of us can stop laughing.

"I don't think there even was," says Lucy. "I think you just saw an opportunity there and took it." Her daughter giggles. I brought a book for each of the kids, and we read them together before they head to bed. With Dad home and the kids readying for bed, Lucy and I hop in the Jammer and drive around. We don't go anywhere, we just wind street after street, sipping Sanpellegrinos and talking and laughing. We eventually settle on a gravel pullout overlooking a field on one side and the end of the airport runway on the other.

"We used to do this all the time near Richmond growing up," Lucy tells me. "Just watch the planes come and go from the airport."

"Yeah, I did that growing up on the island too, but because of the military base it was super cool planes."

"Do you think they all go the same direction?"

"What do you mean?" I ask her, eyeing the airport.

"Like, one of those planes is turning around, but you'd think there'd be one direction for taking off and one for landing . . ."

"Well, yeah, you'd assume they don't have planes landing on a runway one way, and then minutes later planes taking off on a runway the other direction, they must have multiple . . ."

Lucy interrupts my thought with laughter.

"Why are we talking about this? Like I'm going to need to be some expert on planes? Like I need to really have a good handle on the runway situation." I laugh too. We have the windows rolled down so we can smoke, and the occasional mosquito sneaks in and out of the car.

"The mosquitos are bad tonight," I say to her.

"Yeah, but my kid definitely took advantage of the slap scenario," she laughs.

"Oh wait, you know what ... hold on ... I have ..." I reach behind me into the chaos of my backseat and emerge with a citronella candle. Lucy bursts out laughing.

"What the hell, who do you have that?"

"From the night when we camped at the farmhouse." I place it on the dashboard and light it.

"We're getting weirder," I say to her.

"Oh, absolutely, but our weirdness is normal to me."

"Watch this," I say, and I pull from my purse several mini jams and lay them on the dash next to the candle. We're both laughing.

"Are you just wandering around with those in your purse now?"

"Ugh, yeah, obviously."

"When the heart-gina flame burns ..." she jokes but can't finish her sentence because she's laughing so hard, so I jump in.

"When the heart-gina flame is extinguished we must dig up your time capsule." We're both laughing so hard we gasp for breath and keep adding to each other's sentences making the laughter worse and worse and subsequently better and better.

She tells me growing up she and her best friend used to just drive around and smoke cigarettes. I tell her Tese and I did the same.

"You know, she's been gone so long now," I say of Tese, "that she's been gone longer than I knew her. So bizarre."

We talk at length about everything and anything. We talk about how one day the dust will settle, and everything will make sense to us again.

"But, you know," I say, "these messy times, these bad times, these confusing times, like all of the shit I've put myself through and the mistakes that I've made, you never see it at the time, but they make you a person of such deeper substance, and kindness and compassion, and empathy. I hate the road I've taken to get here, but I wouldn't want to change the positive impact on who I am. Things that have happened that have made me closer to you and built the bond I have with your kids . . . wouldn't a had that. Lots of good always comes out of things in the end."

"Nope" says Lucy, who laughs and then says, "the second I said it I knew that wasn't the word I wanted."

"Did you literally just say 'nope' to agree with me?"

"Yes." She's laughing as we pull up to her house. "You're very wise though."

"I didn't get wise by being smart, that's for sure. Talk to you soon."

We linger a bit longer coordinating a schedule for her daughter's graduation from Girl Guides and then I watch her walk inside. At home I read a book about a woman who attempts to truly live by the guidance of several self-help books for an entire year. I fall asleep in the comfort that others are searching too.

I video-chat Mitch because I want to make sure he's OK that I've written about the person connected to him that holed herself up with the decaying corpse. When he answers it's pitch black.

"Hold on," he says, "let me get the light." I always forget that he's one hour ahead of me and probably was in bed. When the light comes on, though, I can tell he wasn't asleep.

"Hi!" I say excitedly. "I just was reviewing my writing and wanted to make sure you'd be good with me including the day you told me about the girl and the body."

"Yeah, yeah, you don't have to check with me about that stuff."

"Ok, I'm just paranoid because I know for some people it's like too personal or whatever. People want their privacy."

"When have I ever had a fucking secret?" he asks me and I laugh. He's right. Between what he shares on stage and in interviews he's about as brutally honest as they come, and I've always admired that about him. "I should learn to keep a fucking secret."

"You OK though?" he asks.

"Yeah, all good, just been writing and working my face off."

"That's good, you're hungry for it."

"Yeah, better than forcing it, for sure. This time I just wrote whenever I felt there was something to write about, so it might be boring, but who the fuck knows."

"Or maybe it'll be even better."

"Maybe." I smile. We chat quickly about some changes to the company who'll be arranging his touring and the reasons for it all. Then when we're wrapping up, he leans in close to the camera and says, "And stop smoking cigarettes. Who the fuck am I kidding, you don't listen to anybody."

I burst out laughing. "Wonder Woman never smoked a fucking cigarette in her life," he says referencing the Wonder Woman hoodie and PJ pants I'm currently wearing. I laugh more.

"K, buddy, just wanted to double check."

"love you," he says.

"Love you too," I tell him. The screen goes dark, and I light a cigarette.

A radio opportunity arises that I simply cannot decline. It's entirely different than anything I've ever done before. First of all, it's normal hours. Pardon me? That's unheard of. I've never had normal hours in my life. Second of all, it's a role that combines several different types of things, all of which excite me. This opportunity is with the gentleman I met with back in March, the one I worked for as a teenager. I like and respect him immensely. He's recently brought on board a new program director whom I find easy to talk to and would be very excited to work with and learn from as well. This opportunity would put me back into the field I love.

"Can I take five minutes, and to be honest, all I want to do is call my dad and run this past him. Yeah, I know . . . I'm that girl."

"Of course," the program director tells me.

"Great, I'll get back to you soon."

"Dad?" I say as his face appears in the frame. He's sitting in the back seat of a cab in Nashville.

"What's up, Bert?"

"I got offered a radio job." I explain the entire thing.

"Awesome!" he tells me. We talk through the role, the hours, the salary, I run him through everything.

"I'd start July third."

"You," he smiles at me, "are a broadcaster, and a damn good one too. You were meant to be on the radio, kid. It's where you shine the brightest. You have so much to offer that industry still. If you trust these people, then take it."

"Imma take it," I say back to him.

"Take it!"

"I'll have to quit the restaurant." I'm caught off guard by how sad this makes me.

"Yeah, you will. From everything you've told me about your boss, though, I think she'll understand."

"I just feel terrible because I told her I was done with radio. I thought I was, ya know?"

"I know. Just do it in person."

"Course. Love you."

"Love you too, and hey, congrats, kid. You earned this."

"Thanks, Dad."

I wander nervously through the restaurant, where she is seated at one of the tables.

"Hi," I say sheepishly.

"Hi. What's up?" She can see right away there is sadness in my face.

"An opportunity came up in radio that I couldn't say no to, and I'm going to take it, so I have to give you my two weeks' notice." Tears sting my eyes. "I'm so sorry, the last thing in the world I wanted to do was disappoint you."

She smiles so warmly.

"It's OK."

"Really?" I ask.

"Absolutely." She brushes the air with her hand in a gentle sweeping motion. "It's fine, these things happen. When you like someone you just want the best for them, and if this is the best thing for you, I'm really happy for you. I want to see people do well regardless of where they do that."

"I just know how much time and patience you've spent on training me, and I feel so badly because you gave me a chance when I needed it and I hold you in such high regard . . ."

"No, no, I understand. You were done with radio, but you weren't done."

"Exactly."

We chat at length about what I've learned in my time working for her. I talk about the amazing impact being part of her world has had on me. How humbling it's been to have been so awful, how much respect I have for her and anyone who can do this type of work. It's a really nice pleasant talk.

"You can still work through Canada Day long weekend though, right? Because we're counting on you."

"Absolutely," I tell her. I feel so elated that she isn't mad at me. I don't think I could take it if someone I admire as much as her felt mistreated by me. I run into Kelly on my way out.

"Hey, what's up?" she asks.

"Ah, I just came in to talk to the boss. Gave my notice."

"No!" she says.

"Yeah, I had something come up in radio again, and I just couldn't say no."

She hugs me and I hug her back super hard.

"I'm so sad because I feel like I was maybe just slowly starting to get the hang of it . . . but . . . the universe takes us where we are meant to be, right?"

"Right."

Scott wanders out from the kitchen with his arms spread wide.

"Roobear, you don't even say hi to me?"

"Sorry, my mind was super hyper-focused on one thing today." I sneak myself into him for a hug. "I came in to give my notice."

"Fuck you," he says jokingly.

"Right? We'll chat more later."

A text comes from Scott a few hours later.

"So, I hope you didn't leave because you're frustrated or think you couldn't get better. Because then I might be mad at you."

"No, no, it wasn't that at all. I'm disappointed I won't be sticking around to attempt to rise to the challenge. I just had an unexpected opportunity come my way that I couldn't decline."

"OK, good, because I really believe personal growth comes from facing adversity. What's the opportunity, you gonna broadcast again?"

"Yeah, can't say much until it's announced publicly, but back to radio."

"Well, good for you, man. Get super famous so I can steal more of your Instagram followers."

"Bahahaha," I send back. I hope he knows I'm going to hold on to him and Kelly, and that my leaving doesn't give them an out on friendship. I daydream about the new job. My heart twinkles when I think of radio control rooms and beautiful soundboards with buttons that light up. I think maybe the way car fanatics feel when they look at whatever type of vehicle really does it for them is the same awe I feel staring at audio equipment. I picture myself happy and with headphones on. I picture myself in front of a computer editing audio again. I see myself doing the things I believe I was born to do. I wonder if I'll have a little desk somewhere. Will there be room to put a frame on it? What would I put, some pictures of me and Lucy and the kids? Jer and I? Greyson? The "family" photo of me with Jer and Hendrik and Roxy? I can't tell you how many times I've seen radio employees come and go with boxes, starting or leaving, filled with certificates of merit or the occasional award. I will not be bringing any of my awards to this new job. I think what I will do is frame my waitressing pouch. It seems like a perfect tribute to what I've learned this last year. It seems like the perfect reminder of humility and hard work, of the me I have found, that I never ever ever want to lose again.

Chapter 24

Conclude the Interlude

I was continuously worried during the writing of this book that I wouldn't know when it was supposed to be done. This "interlude." Defined as "an intervening or interruptive period, space, or event: interval." I feel in my heart my "interlude" has now concluded.

There's a children's book called *The Monster at the End of this Book*. My father used to read it to me as a child. It's Grover from *Sesame Street*, and he tells you right off the hop, "Don't turn the page, because there's a monster at the end of this book." So naturally, you turn the page, and watch out, because Grover starts getting serious. He builds a wall with sticks, and then with bricks, and at each page he cautions you more and more severely, "Stop going, there's a monster at the end of this book!" Well, spoiler alert, at the very end he realises it's him. He is the monster at the end of the book. I have been the monster of my own story time and time again. All this time I've been fighting what I perceived to be some external force that inhibited me for truly moving on and finding my new "normal." I have been fighting only myself, my perceptions of myself, my grief, my fear, my guilt, my anxiety, my decisions, my beliefs. I am the monster. Nothing has ever held me back but myself, and now that I acknowledge this, I am free. I am free to live where I want, I am free to work where I want, I am free to love whomever I want. I am not only free, but I also understand that I have been waiting for someone to tell me when my life has "begun" again, as if it's simply been on pause. Jesus Christ! What was I thinking? This interlude has been life! Some of the hardest, messiest, saddest most hilarious life, but life, nonetheless.

As I sat down to write this today my Google Play was streaming me a randomly suggested list of music, like always. A song came on that I had never heard before. I stopped and replayed it several times, leaning back in my chair, closing my eyes, and just listening to the words over and over. The song is Kina Grannis "In the Waiting." I go back to the beginning of this book and place an excerpt of the lyrics right at the start. "And all this time, I've been staring at the minute hand, oh what a crime! That I can't seem to understand, that life is in the waiting." Oh man, oh fuck, it's just true. Life is in the waiting. I have been waiting and waiting and waiting for my life to start again. It never stopped. Thank God, for this beautiful interlude.

ACKNOWLEDGMENTS

Thank you to you. Yeah YOU. Thank you for supporting my crazy dream by reading this book. The magnitude of personal responses I received after the release of my first book truly astounded me. I do not take the time you have spent consuming my words for granted, and it is an honor to be invited into your life in this way. Thank you for the safe space you've created in your hearts, your bookshelves and your homes, for me to share such deeply personal thoughts and feelings.

Lucy, I trust you implicitly. You can trust me completely, absolutely, totally, wholeheartedly, utterly, unconditionally, unreservedly, and always. I can't promise I won't fuck up, but when I do, I'll always move mountains to make it right. You give me a home, a family, and most of all a best friend. I'll always throw my pack on to hike the trail with you, and I'm sorry for the times I make us bushwhack . . . the easy route is boring anyways. Let's spend our lives building snowmen, hiding jam, and very very very occasionally letting the drawbridges down so someone else can visit our castle. (Watch out for the moat, it has both sharks and alligators.) Let's always respond to being told we can't do something, by cutting down a tree. I cannot do this without you, and I'm so very lucky that I never have to.

Greyson, you've turned chaos into order, and I admire and respect you so much for that. ("New concept!") Thank you for everything you have done for me. You know I've been "lizard" wrong about a lot of things in my lifetime, but the high regard I continue to hold you in will never be one of them. Your conviction, your truth, your support, your . . . on and on and on . . . all the thoughts, none of the words, but you know . . . I know you know. Love to the Floof always. Baby dinosaurs for life.

James, please continue to be happy in the world and pursue the things and people that you love, because watching you get it right fills my heart with joy. I love watching you love and be loved. I want only the best for you and your family forever. Dogs send many mlems.

Seamus, a friendship is not defined by the good moments, because those are easy. It's found in the turmoil, it's forged in the frustration, and defined only by how we rise from these moments to love each other even when it seems impossible to do so. You've shown me forgiveness and humility, and most of all provided the space I needed when I needed it. Letting someone have the space, the chance, the right . . . to be dead wrong . . . that's not easy. But you make it look easy. I love you brother.

Jer, Roxy and Hendrik, all the love and appreciation, all the time, always.

Meesh, no matter how many days or months pass, we pick back up where we left off, and you meet me with the deepest understanding and compassion. I appreciate you so much and I love watching you bring what you do to the world.

Scott, thanks for lending your skills again, and for reminding me not to have video chats on unsecure platforms.

Brooks, you are amazing and none of this is possible without your help and talents. You're the best friend I've never met.

And finally, to the boy next door, thank you for leaving me tulips, which, in turn, started it all.

Made in the
USA
Lexington, KY